Chat

The First Year on the Internet

by K. Allen

published by Flying Finish Press

ISBN 978-0-6151-6356-7

to my many friends
and
chat buddies

4

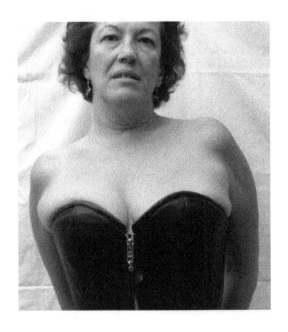

You may know me by my infamous *Имя интернета*.
In any case, you're in for a wild ride.

The authoress neither confirms nor denies the veracity of anything contained in this book. As is so often the case with the Internet, enter at your own risk.

6

Please note:
Everyone's Name/Handle/Designation
has been carefully removed to protect
the Not-So-Innocent.

Are you sitting comfortably?
then
Let us begin....

APRIL
2005

04/05/2005
'Ware! This lady has 'Control Issues'

04/07/2005
Dancing to the tune of "Clubbed to Death" from The Matrix !! He didn't seem to mind.

04/09/2005
POLO POLO POLO - Friday and Saturday evenings are beginning to book up! Catch us if you can!

04/14/2005
Mmmmmm life continues to be 'interesting'. The IRS, love them!, is giving us back some money. Party time!!!

04/16/2005
"Twas brilig and the slithy toves" but appreciating the wicked subtleties of life is truly gratifying. Chortling!!

04/17/2005
Terribly sorry to disappoint you all but you cannot rule the world for I already do.

04/19/2005
We have met a great many wonderful people since we have joined. Thank you all for welcoming us.

04/20/2005

For in flight entertainment we offer involuntary extreme aerobatics guaranteed to keep your interest! For you timid flyers, we promise, really we will, to check the weather beforehand.

04/21/2005

Yes, it is nice to be added to a wish list and yes, we do check out your profile - we will reply yeah or nay. Which is the entire point of having the wish list since so many people dislike 'pushy' people - the wish list is a gentle way of saying ' May I?' . The next move is up to the Wish list Add-ee. You say you want to meet people? Here's your chance!

04/22/2005

It looked like summer for a few days there! So I did get outside for a little while. Now it seems it is time for payment. Rain and back to 50 degree weather. Ick! Time to curl up with some scotch and a few good men!!!

04/23/2005

I limped past a small group of people who asked me to donate and sign a petition against violence, I did, laughing inwardly, as my limping was the result of my own violent passions - yeah, I know, I know - I'm not 18 anymore, but there's something about men that just ignites my engines.

04/24/2005,
Hilarious, and slightly confused - a GREAT party !!
Thank you for inviting us !! Only thing to add is
"More sex, please - we're NOT British." Btw, we do
have to leave by midnight so don't hang back -
tackle us with enthusiasm as soon as we walk in the
door.

04/26/2005
I have relented! Okay so we will stay longer and
NOT leave at midnight but still, by all means, still
tackle us with enthusiasm as soon as we walk in the
door! Not even unreasonable offers will be refused!

04/27/2005
As an experiment, and since the Wishlist seems to
generate about as much response as yesterday's
dead fish, we posted a Playtime note. Well, we
received one interested but can't, one couple who
never showed, and one - just the one, single man.
He's dream though so it worked out. Other recent
experiments include listing our social schedule on
the Calendar which has also generated no response
and hanging out in the Chat being very, very shy
and timid. We do get invited to parties however,
and they are usually very fun indeed! Come on
people! I don't bite......well, only a little.

04/29/2005

Siempre Reparatan Pecunia = SRP for all of those who did NOT ask. Although Always Purple Gerbils was very good, I still prefer Aesthetically Pleasing Gardeners. OH MY!. I am so excited about this weekend! Lots of frolicking will occur and you know how I love a good frolic! Unfortunately, my rad houseparty outfit will take 8 to 10 weeks to make so you will just have to endure my leathers once more. Polo begins May 21st BYOB - if you want to come (cum?) just let us know. We will swing by and 'pick you up'! Pun more than merely intended. ON my quest to find suitable lap dancing music, the Deftones' Lucky You has been added to the list. Morissette's Fear of Bliss has also been added but provisionally. If you know of any tunes that will go with these, including Rob Dugan's Clubbed to Death, please send them along. Thank you.

04/30/2005

The search for suitable dancing music continues!!! To those who sent in suggestions, thank you for trying! Thus far we have the Deftones' Lucky You, R. Dugan's Clubbed to Death and Morissette's Fear of Bliss - am checking out the Deftones' Deathblow to see if it will fit in. Any DJ's, amateurs included, may contribute their suggestions. I need spooky, slow hip twitching, "will he survive the night" music. Who knows, I may give you a dance using the cd we create!!! We were rained out so no Wine Fest for us. I hope that the 'golf' scheduled for tomorrow actually occurs. Wish me luck! Last Friday's houseparty was FUN, FUN, FUN !!! Thank you to all of you wonderful people !!! Please don't be strangers !!!

MAY
2005

05/01/2005

Thank you your dance music suggestions! Very kind and yes, I will list the songs. It has been an interesting day. All I can say is I am going to have one mind-blowing retirement !!! You guys are the greatest !!!

05/03/2005

Can someone explain to me why I am having more fun now than when I was 20? Can it be that evil devil-women need older men who don't scare easily?

05/04/2005

I agree - people if you must drive slowly, do it over there! Not in front of me!!! If you see a large white object hurtling up onto your rear bumper - well now you know who it is. Please scoot over. This won't take a moment. Thank you very much.

05/08/2005

Dance music update: current playlist is R. Dugan's Clubbed to Death, Deftone's Lucky You, Sisters of Mercy's Ribbons, Rammstein's Stripped, Deftone's Deathblow and Sisters of Mercy's Lucretia my Reflection and Flood 1. I am also considering some Nine Inch Nails, Slipknot and Type O Negative. What do you think of including the song "Tainted Love"?

16

05/09/2005

The Bull Run Hunt Point to Point races down in Culpepper, VA were tremendous fun! And now I am all pink! Unfortunately I only had the one winner - Hurray, Road Hazard !!! I did get cheese in my hair. Sorry, none of you guys came along so no pix for you! Ha ha ha ha ha! And so, back to work.

05/10/2005

Ever notice how that four letter word that begins with w interferes with a good sex life? Ah well, I do have several credit card companies relying upon my support - they need me so I guess I shall continue to tread the path even as the office cat silently laughs at me and my efforts to keep her in catnip mice. But I would very much rather be sitting next to you in the twilight on the deck slowly getting drunk on scotch while listening to Janis Joplin singing 'Summertime'.

05/14/2005

Party or Polo? There's no choice here. PARTY!!! Thank you for inviting us! Ladies - he's all yours! I actually to a dance out of him last night at the Taj!! Guys - the Devil-woman is out tonight. Let us hope you are up to it! Now playing Sisters of Mercy's Lucretia my Reflection, and similar, at sound level marked "puree'" as I clean the house in an extremely miniscule thong bikini. BTW - does anyone know how to effectively prune Scotch Broom?

05/16/2005

Wonderful Silk & Skin this past Saturday! Thank you to all of you lovely people! I wasn't in top form and so did not get to 'meet' all of the men - but I did try, I assure you! Am tossing Cat onto the tender mercies of the ladies! I am off - temp only. See you all later! The scotch broom remains un-pruned! And the lap dance cd remains incomplete! Just too much to do! KISSES

05/18/2005

Such a serious bunch ! How did it ever come to this? There is simply not enough hilarity in this world! Here is my contribution to help you all along further down the path of group giggles: picture in your mind - 2am at the top of the stairs where there's not enough room to breathe, a naked 6'4" man with a broom and a cat entwined around his ankles, trying to swat a squeaking bat, the cat is yelling up instructions, it is dark and he's trying to NOT fall down the stairs, trip over the cat, or wake the kids! - I get the most interesting phone calls at work! Here's another: another phone call "Mom! There's a van in the living room!" "A van?!?!?" "Yes, the van, you know, in the living room." "How did a van get our living room?" and then the standard kid response (repeat after me) "I don't know." Yegods! and there are people who want kids?? That call led to a quick dash home!

05/19/2005

Shaving, breast augmentation, tummy tucks; why not, since you're gonna why dontcha, get a couple of ribs removed? Then , since fair is fair, we women can start in on having men made to our specifications as well! PFFFT! Such silliness! Lets go and play naked bar badminton instead! Where two or more person in chairs, castors help, and a glass in one hand, try to keep a shuttlecock in the air without spilling their drink or falling out of their chairs. The fun is increased if the dart players have their game set up perpendicular to the badminton game. And here you thought I didn't know how to have fun! Loser(s) buy. NB: the above was an accurate portrayal of an actual event and some dart players were a big help as they assisted with batting shuttlecocks periodically

05/21/2005

Body odor? Nothing major here, just make running through the shower first part of your sexy routine! Some sweet smelling soap and a scrubbing poofy thing - you can have fun with this - and body odor is a thing of the past! Sorry about your hair and makeup but the gas mask would have ruined your look anyway. Or not! I remember three of us getting into our gas masks, lining up and line dancing to the tune Wild Thing; combat boots doing a stomp! Have pictures to prove it too! We looked so cute in our cami jammies!

05/22/2005
You all missed a great, if damp, time at the polo field yesterday! We had lots of fun and the food was good too! We have two free passes for next week's games so get with us if you'd care to go! We trim, we do not shave. And now I must dive back into Tax Planning *ker splash!*

05/23/2005
"eye of newt and toe of frog; wool of bat and tongue of dog. Fillet of a finney snake in the pot to boil and bake." I think I will stick to my diet, thank you very much! Drove up to and back from Penn State today and I need one of those drinks known as a 'corpse-raiser' and a massage with scented oils performed by one very, very nice male. Fortunately, I have both in stock and at hand! I hope all of you enjoy your evening as much as I am going to! Ooooooooo baby! Yes. Right there! Aaaaaaaaaaaah!

05/25/2005
"love lost, fire at will; dum-dum bullets and shoot to kill." such a jumping tune too! Hello, my darlings!! When did you all become so prissy? Tis penis, testicles, vagina and breasts. And long may they all wave! The best way to add elegance to a man's living room sofa is for a lady to lounge naked upon it! (And vice versa!) Nevermind - am just feeling my oats this morning! Trying to get the maximum out of every second! ROTBLMAO

05/26/2005

Hmmmm.. logically if MEAN PEOPLE SUCK then ...some of the people who suck MUST, of necessity, be mean. Are you one of THEM? Should we be on the look-out for you? LOOK BEHIND YOU!!!! Oh, Sorry! Didn't mean to interrupt you two! Carry on! I will just step over here and ooze quietly away. Now then, who haven't I had the pleasure of? Ah! There's a naked man on my sofa! I love volunteers! Esp furry ones. MMMMMMMMMMmmmmmmmm Now , now. Just lie back and do whatever the not-so-nice lady says, darling. Heh, heh, heh.

05/27/2005

Can you say from whence these quotes came? 1. "That dog, I say, that dog is lower than a snake full of buckshot." 2. "Silly me, that was my sweeping broom!" 3. "Would I do this if my friend Rocky was in there?" 4. "Never hit the red button!" and last but not least we have The Wilston Green Underwater Knitting Society and The Car Park Attendant's Latin American Dance Team! Two very fine organizations if I say so myself. HELP, HELP I am being repressed! And after the spanking...the oral sex! What I actually did say last night was "go get naked and lie down."

JUNE
2005

06/02/2005

And the answers are: 1. Foghorn Leghorn; 2. Witch Hazel; 3. Bugs Bunny; 4. Daffy Duck. The Wilston Green Underwater Knitting Society and The Car Park Attendant's Latin American Dance Team are from the English cartoon series Dangermouse; then we have Monty Python's Holy Grail. The final quotation was what I said last night.

06/03/2005

For those who do not know, Cat of Catnip is the male (yummmy!) and Nip is the female (I suppose I will do) - and no, I am not bi in the least tyvm. Yes, we smoke like those old locomotives, drink scotch but lightly and fornicate like sex-starved rabbits. We are also unshaved because I prefer fur. Any problems with that? I also have 'control issues' but I am reasonably well-behaved about it - you can ask Cat. All we ask is please be aggressive, ardent, talkative, and fun! We will do our best to make you cum so hard that you fall off the bed! Careful there, you almost hit the nightstand! Here, come and snuggle, hun.

06/04/2005

I think we missed you last night there at the Taj! It was so crowded and noisy that we may have been obscured from eachother - we tried to keep a look out but you know how it can be. We apologize and hope that you will give us another opportunity. Did you enjoy yourselves nevertheless? You had wanted to get out for while after all.

06/05/2005

To tan or not to tan, well you all know my answer to that *w* hang around a swimming pool full of water in the bright sun for hours at a time and a farmer's tan you will have my little chickadee! Now me, I just smear on something or other and hang out on the library deck nude during the weekdays cause you all know the suburbs are empty during the week. This is also good for drying nail polish - if it doesn't rain. Should you have any questions *waving a huge book around* it is all here in "Aunt Agatha's Answers" so feel free to ask. I am especially fond of the entry concerning nose approximations of Jovian whistlers myself.

06/06/2005

Oh dear! It seems I have been a little too rough on these tender and delicate men. Sorry fellas but I got carried away - ya know how that is? Notice to all future playmates: No I will NOT wear gloves but I will make a valiant attempt to leave you intact. I promise! See? My fingers aren't even crossed! Ooooops! *hiding claws* (Forgot to take those off.) Just pretend you didn't see them, ok? Sorry about your knee, S! I shall have to restrict throwing myself into the masculine arms of those males strong enough to catch me. *eg* It is going to be a rough week for Cat!

06/08/2005

It seems we need some feedback. Deal breaking has been going on - oh, we can set appts but then they are not kept for a variety of reasons, or in this case, without any sort of reason whatsoever, *sigh* very disheartening! Is it me? Yes, it is being a rough week for Cat. All the poor man does is work and then 'work'! Is there such a thing as too much fun?

06/09/2005

Twas brilig and the slithy toves and so goes another dinner out with friends followed by a small misunderstanding and Cat's in trouble once more! Or is that Nip's in trouble once more? It is one of those 'but I told you' / 'no you didn't tell me' things often experienced by couples where feminine elliptical reference, and he's expected to knit information together, meets masculine inability to multi-task information over a period of months. And exactly when is our anniversary, dear? So before Cat gets dried eye of newt in his morning coffee - someone hand him some knitting needles.

06/11/2005

I am one disgruntled kitten - it is a lovely day and I am housecleaning?!?! There's no justice in this world!!

06/13/2005

Justice has returned to the world!! Spent the day motorcycling on Skyline Drive in the Shenandoah National Park!! Saw deer, tiger swallowtail butterflies, and one wild turkey. Beautiful day! Now the happy kitten will go and lounge in the hot tub - naked of course! HAPPY BIRTHDAY, S!!!

06/14/2005

Another lovely day -man how I do love summer !!! Shame about work though. Ah, well. Am trying to get more music onto my Seduction cd, also trying to get through this course - anyone want to play proctor?, and also trying to get all home videos onto dvd - no they aren't all THAT kind of video tyvm. Not that we don't have any of those, mind you. And I really, really, REALLY should tidy up my office *eg* seems to have gotten way out of hand lately. You don't think I have too many projects do you?? Excuse me but I have letters to get out, people to call and two packages to have FedEx pick up. Yes we want to play with you - just trying to find the time!!! BTW we prefer smaller house parties where we know people - not those big bash things, where we don't know anyone.

06/15/2005

Separate rooms or same room tis all the same to me, hun! I am not a small and fragile lady *eg* as some of you can attest. No, no - I am cute and timid little woodland creature! *batting eyelashes* (heh, heh, heh) Now that I have inveigled you into my world, how about a kiss? I won't bite...........at least.................not yet. *w* (That comes later.) Ah the joys of summer! One of which is running around scantily clad! Ooooooooo baby! I was out and about buzzing in my MGB yesterday. Man, I really, really, REALLY LOVE THAT CAR! The top is down, the music is up and the roads weren't too bad. At least I wasn't sitting there stationary with thousands of my closest friends. I used my supersecrethoneybunny route to get home with all of its twists and turns! WOW! What fun! Have your people call my people and I'll take you for a ride. *wicked evil grin fading ala Cheshire*

06/16/2005
While watching her beloved husband roll about on the floor wrestling with their kids, the lady has only one thing to say - "The lamp!! Watch out for the lamp!!!" Happy Father's Day to all of you reproductively successful males out there! And please, be careful of the furnishings. *eg* For some reason the horns on the MGB are now stuck. Had to pull the connections to get the horns (there are two of them) to shut down. Hmmmm. *image of woman pondering the innards under the hood* I prefer the noise to be due to engines and exhausts not horns. *screwing down the caps on the twin SU carbs* I wonder why its doing that. *topping off the oil* Oh and I have just about finished my Evil Seduction cd. Only 6 minutes and some odd seconds left. *image of woman now calling up Ken the MGB mechanic* HELP!!!!

06/17/2005
Friday and we are off to Chetwood Farm for polo !!! Talk about a romp !! Have new music for the truck, yes the Evil Seduction cd is finished !! Email for the list if you want it. I was out again in my MGB. Terror stalking the street! Nip's out driving !!! If you see old people diving over hedges you will know I have just passed them! Sidewalks?!?! What sidewalks?!? Well, at least the lovely police like me. I contribute so much to their coffers. Cat will vouch that I haven't killed anyone all week! Looking forward to the weekend and all of you darling people! Promise I will miss you. Really I will.

06/19/2005

Having missed all of you during my weekend's driving, told you I would, I am now in the house diligently studying away like a good little kitten. For those following our adventures, Friday's polo match final score was 4 to 3 Yellow team won. Cat missed the lady in the Mercedes trying to remove her new nipple ring without taking her shirt and bra off - man, was he disappointed when I told him about it! Apparently it was causing her some distress. It was very nice to see our host finally, but his health is improving now so we expect to see more of him. One might expect my vehicle to be overawed by all of those Jags and Mercs but this is a 2004 Ford F150 with every bell and whistle known to mankind in pristine condition so if the guys didn't drool over me, they were drooling over my truck. For those of you keeping count, I have 7 vehicles and Cat has 2. Heh, heh, heh - we can sneak up on you without you knowing its us.

06/20/2005

Being one of those who hit the ground running, I can tell you that the foreplay begins as soon as the invitation is received so lets not waste time. This is understandable since sex begins in the mind. Not today, however, since I have to test on Taxation but just you wait! Now I am not saying that five year look back recapture, depreciation schedules, and cost recovery does it for me; but passing the test will! Triumph has that effect! Wish me well, gals and guys! (my proctor is very cute!) Wonder how I look in my orange thong bikini? Some will find out this weekend! Thank you for the invite! We are looking forward to it!

06/21/2005

Ah! Time for some Zen....lounging on the library deck, sipping something cool, listening to Janis sing "Summertime", as the sun washes over my skin. Hey! Just because I have to hang by the phone today doesn't mean I don't know how to do it with style. *eg* The hydrangea are beginning to bloom along with the tiger lilies. Life is so good! BTW the song we requested at the Taj during prom night was "Love You to Death" by Type O Negative. Heavy metal Goth as a slow dance, you would have thought it impossible. It can be done! Now then, if any couples are up for a week night romp, let Cat know. We will see what we can do. Yes, I will behave myself and leave my 'control issues' at home; you gentlemen need have no fears. I promised Cat that I would be a good little kitten..............for now.

06/22/2005

Dental floss?!?! How long are we talking here? My 1/4 to 1/2 inch fur isn't going to clean anyone's interspacials. They make it sound like its hanging down to her kneecaps. Please end the controversy before further examples of my sense of humor escape me. And yes I like the tiered system of payments - it gives me hope for the future. It also seems to me that if you are ranting about this sort of thing, you aren't getting enough playtime! If you were getting enough, esp from us, you would be far too exhausted to be able to type, let alone rant. And, finally, I am not the sort of woman who gets groped in any case because they fear their offer just might be taken up and they'd find themselves on their backs (thud!) without any introduction at all. You will recall my unfortunate habit of hurtling myself into masculine arms. Yes, see, I knew you remembered. Begin at the ankles, boys, and slowly lick your way up! Now isn't that better than getting all aggro in the blog? Yes. Oooo, that tickles!

06/23/2005
Here I thought it was the person who mattered and NOT the packaging! Read their profile and they aren't playful, racist perhaps but definitely not playful. But the sun is out, the day is warm, and there are much more interesting people in the world so no need to waste any time lingering over such as they have proven to be. Packed two weeks worth of groceries into my MGB and ran out of room for the beer!! Bad kitty! But it was fun driving it all home! No, I didn't lose anything when I went around the corners on two wheels. Will have to have the Beer Fairy bring some home for Cat. The poor man is beer-less and we cannot have that! Naturally there is never any shortage of scotch. Hmmmm. I seem to be out of books to read. A trip to the library is also called for then. Beer and books! Sounds like a nice 'snuggleable' evening at home!

06/24/2005
Lets see: polo and the Taj then a boat party and then a quiet Sunday recuperating at British Car Day. Shame we don't get out much! All this and my daughter reverts to being boneheaded again! Yegods! Wants to run off, live with her bf and go to college, yeah right, on her own not very existent dime down in AL when she's already been accepted at one very fine school in VA. Argh! I shall have to point out that its a 'running from' rather than a 'running toward' - well, this is why parents are paid

the big bucks, right? I work to relieve the stress of home and have home to relieve the stress of work. No wonder none of you men are safe from me!

06/26/2005
Had a marvelous boat ride yesterday hence no blog entry. Shame about some people but what can one do? Had fun today as well! Nice cars and even got to motorcycle a bit! Then painted the crowns on our English telephone booth in gold leaf whilst wearing my orange thong bikini. The same one as yesterday. There were people home today so could not wear the miniscule version of the same. They would have seen me!!! *gasp* All very nicely brown here! Now to go and tackle Cat!

06/27/2005
And so the week begins! Unfortunately, it looks like a damp and dreary one. Cat has to go off for a couple of days as well. Both of which make me rather irritable. Guess I shall just have to work; trying to be the person all of the alternate lifestyle people go to, you see. None of this 'you need funding for what?!?!?' LOL However, I still have one day before he leaves to really enjoy Cat. Will plan to make the most of the opportunity. Perhaps some pix?

06/28/2005
Triggers to get turned on? Hmmmm. Well, for me the foreplay begins when the invitation is received but it takes Cat a little longer. Hearing me usually works for him *eg*. And nothing you do or say ignites, guys, it is something about the line of your neck into your shoulder, the way you stand and move - indefinables that catch me. Overt interest

doesn't hurt but the gleaming eye does the trick. Have I mentioned teddybears? I have this thing for teddybears esp ones with those cute little devil horns poking up through their fur. Mmmmmm, fur!! So now you know.

06/29/2005

Compliments?!?! Wheeeeeeeeee, compliments!!! Love it and thank you, thank you, thank you! *happy dance* I am just sooo shy. I am lost without my teddybear!! He should return sometime tonight. I hope he's as hungry as I am!! *w* Perhaps I shall purrrrr at him to get him going? I shall have to tidy up first - amazing how women turn into slackers when their males are absent. Brush my fur, paint my claws, sharpen my fangs. Change the sheets? Hmmmm. "Evil. Evil." You won't tell, will you?

06/30/2005

Cat's back and why is it that peeps keep their hotel rooms so damn cold - he's caught a chill! So instead of 'ahem' I have to nurse him back to health! Now proceeding to bake him; lets see 350 for 30 minutes then turn over and bake for a further 15 minutes. Cool. We will see if that works. If not, I will have to use more drastic measures. *w* Ah! The timer just went off. Sorry but I have to run and turn him over! What do you think? Basting?

JULY
2005

07/01/2005

I hate shorts! No, no - not those cute things men wear around their haunches, but those electrical things that zap your auto. Yes my wonderful MGB broke down! I called for rescue! There he came! My knight in shiny Yukon bearing 5-30 oil and a jumpstart; or two, or three until it finally dies on the way to the mechanic. (Ken. You will remember him from an earlier entry.) Bet the alternator is fried. Need a new battery too. My darling Cat rescued me and then took care of my grave emotional trauma by feeding me scotch and giving me rolling orgasms. This was after the oil btw. Ken should call soon and mention something in the region of $1 million 6 to fix the MGB and he will undoubtedly want that in rubles. This means I shall have to get my purse. (The supersecrethunnybunny purse that always has just what you need in it.) So for now my 7 vehicles have become 6 - oh, whatever shall I do?

07/02/2005

We empathize with you having been there and 'not done' that? Fuck parties are the greatest but only if everyone comes prepared to fuck anything that breathes! Now I, of course, am very timid and shy about sex. Just ask anyone who knows me. Someone called the cops once. Oh! and Ken, the mechanic, you remember me mentioning him, called to say that $1 million six in rubles isn't very much and it will cost more. The tow guy came, finally - I had time to paint my claws, and it was cute when he told the car to stay and then indicated to the car that it should hop up onto the jerr-dan tow platform. The car did not respond but we got it up there and it was so sad watching it ride away to Ken's garage. Got the boy from college for the 4th but had to take the 'supersecrethunnybunny' route home as 95 was a parking lot - again. Not too bad of a drive! Happy Fourth and your thanks, I am a veteran, are appreciated. I pass my own on to those both before and after me!

07/03/2005
Nip's Drunk Story - Passed out on the top bunk fully dressed with all sheets etc. on the bed while kissing this cute guy. Woke up completely naked and slightly damp, on the bottom bunk without any sheets etc. which were in a sodden heap on the floor behind the bedroom door. There was a glass of milk in the bathroom sitting on the toilet tank. Your guess is as good as mine. I am not sure that I really want to know.

07/05/2005
Ah, fireworks! I am very fond of watching them soar and explode! That thump whoosh bang! WOW! Had a great deal of fun contributing our allotted amount of black powder/cordite to the festivities! The final tally was no one injured, nothing undesignated burnt, and no authorities descending upon us. We are troublemakers merely disguised as adults, I fear. Either that or we have our pyromania under control. Something auto-viral seems to be going around though. Cat's vehicles have begun acting up! The Yukon's spewing oil and the Honda has one flat tire. Back to the shop! And the Expedition is moaning - a new sound - from something in its drivetrain. Only 200k on the clock - nothing lasts anymore! Still awaiting Ken's call on the MGB. Last month the problems were w testicles - this month it's w tires.

07/06/2005

Ken has called and the alternator - naughty alternator! - has been replaced and my MGB is back in action!!! It didn't cost $1million six in rubles either so that was good! Now the new HD is in for its 1000 mile tweaking and the Yukon is getting a seal/gasket replaced and new oil added. The tire was repaired so the Honda has all of its feet working. All of which is good as we have a boat party coming up! I would not have the required energy if I had to bicycle my way to it. Have tried on my summer dresses and WOW got great reviews - the vanilla men loved it and their vanilla wives hated it! How cool is that? *eg* My best buddy thought it looked great but a trifle beachy for Woodbridge. Cat was having a bit of trouble with his hands - keeping them to himself proved to be too difficult for him. Now to find some sandals to match! SHOPPING!!!!!

07/07/2005

Spent today out and about in my truck which seems to have put itself into four wheel drive - Hmmmm - more trips to the mechanics? Got in all of the groceries, dropped Cat off at his mechanic for the Yukon and went the Silver Ridge Farm for my 1/4 of a cow - a hind quarter, naturally. This month certainly seems to be vehicle trouble month! Hope the boat this weekend holds up! I also hope the weather holds up too! Would be nice to see and bask in the sun again! I would no more ask to see the guest list than I would fly! If he's there and he's breathing - hell he's in with a chance! I prefer keeping within my age cohort but one never knows one's luck so give him his opportunity - he may surprise you! I do so get tired of being the only lady to pull my own weight however. My opinion, and it is only an opinion, is that saying no defeats the purpose of being there which is to fuck, then fuck, and then to fuck some more. Unfortunately, some men can outrun me and they manage to escape! DRAT! However, as I am trying to arrange something, it is a surprise, I will have to let you go and read another's blog. So much to do!

07/08/2005
No politics please! Or we'll never get out of here in time to enjoy some silken dalliance! I think polo will be cancelled for today so we may not be at the TAJ - we shall see how it goes. My last house party was BYOB - as in 'bring your own boy' to share, of course. I invited only women. Who they bought along was up to them and we got some really sweet males brought in! Mmmmmm, very yummy! The weather is supposed to clear up for tomorrow's boat party - I do hope so! The last one was such fun! And I need fun as my daughter remains being bone-headed. *sigh* But you don't want to hear about that. Now it may be true that I will fuck any male that breathes but bear in mind that I will only keep the best. Culling the herd through performance testing I believe its called. No I don't put those little buttons in their ears ala Steiff so its no good searching for one! Mmmmmm furry teddybears! Oh dear! Now look what you've done! You've gotten me distracted!

07/09/2005
Amazing how nice it is to be out on the water with some very good friends! We enjoyed our boat trip enormously!!! Cat and I are both a trifle more pink than when we left but it was worth it! Two missed

the boat and we are sorry to have missed them as they are also very fun. With all of the fun sun and fresh air - we may have to 'nap' *eg* Tomorrow is landscaping, washing floors and other assorted household things. Yes, we do have fun at home too. My iPod's being difficult, hmmmm, and the Expedition's problem turns out to be a split tailpipe. All of this technology! Well, if it isn't one thing - its another! Rather than worrying about it, I think I will go and tackle Cat - again! tee heeeeeeeee

07/11/2005

Had fun trimming bushes - yes, I really do mean actual shrubbery! LOL But I will forgive you if you thought I meant something else! I am dismayed to hear that there are ladies who feel shy about saying "No. Sorry, hun, but no thank you very much." Of course getting up to visit the ladies' room works well too. Me? I just growl and toss them aside. I have my devil woman rep to maintain you see. ROTBL Speaking of which...I haven't tried you, yet now have I? What's up with that? Don't worry, the marks will fade away within 24hrs. Just ask Cat. *eg* Its how I keep track during these house/boat/hotel parties. Call them all 'darling' and mark them so you know you've been there! Sorry, but I have been having far too much fun to take this all so seriously! Ah! I hear a Cat meowing! C Y' ALL

07/12/2005

One book?!?! You neophytes! Have recently read, Retirement Planning and Employee Benefits, The Three Richards, 6 books by Philip R. Craig and 4 by Rett MacPherson (murder mysteries) and the 2005

40

Us Tax Code Guide - talk about heavy going!! Next up are several other murder mysteries and Mad Dogs and Scotsmen - if you haven't read Gerald Hammond you should be ashamed of yourselves. Hmmm I am running out of books again!!! TO THE LIBRARY!!! Have also finished The One Thing as well which was sent to me free by my lawyers. Nice people, my lawyers. They keep me out of trouble. You will hardly ever find me without a book close to hand. Instead of just waiting I wait and read. The new Harry Potter is due out - yes I read them too. Harry makes my jaws ache - he's so diffident it hurts! Needs the rabbit to yell SOCK 'EM, SMOKEY!! Time for Cat's workout!! Guess I should put this book down dontcha think?

07/13/2005
Yes, well, but good looks don't exactly hurt. It's nice when a great person comes in an attractive package but hey! Its how the world goes. Sorry but I actually have to work this morning - amazingly, yes, I do work. I know, I know, I appear so much the lady of leisure who talks of inconsequential things and the fluffy hunnybunny look is a great disguise but it is just a cover story. My hair needs touching up and I did break a couple of claws recently. I have to clear my desk because there's something on for tomorrow afternoon and early evening and then polo and TAJ for Friday and some people trying to entice us down to Charlotte's ville on Saturday and they are vying with the people in Baltimore. And my boneheaded daughter is planning on moving out just after Grandmom comes to visit for several days before and after her little trip to Louisiana and just after I get back from a

weekend at the shore by myself because, jeeez!, I need the rest!!!

07/14/2005

Block someone? No. Have never felt the need to block anyone. Perhaps being a devil-woman helps? "Caution: dangerous person within." I do have a very nice line of invective I could employ. Oh well! Time to move along, move along, nothing to see here. Back to the benefits of defined contribution plans from the employer's perspective! I have been informed that there is entirely too much humor in my household! Cannot think where they got that idea! We are the most staid of people! Very stodgy too. *hiding the leather straps, cuffs etc in the bottom drawer.* No, no - not us! We are very dull and boring. All we do is work, work, work! Speaking of which - perhaps I had better do some. Big afternoon and evening tonight - being dull and stodgy! *eg*

07/15/2005

Kissing? Mmmmmm Love it! Kids in the house? Well, not so much. Would seem to be similar to sex in public places - the old 'hope we don't get caught' thing which is akin to the 'hope the parents don't hear us' thing. I can see your point but it depends upon how you handle such interruptions. Like answering your cell phone during a fuckfest when you are beneath three men. Not that I would know anything about that. Oh no! Not me! *eg* Thank you, Cat! I have been informed that my summer dresses look 'absolutely smashing' on me by a very nice Kiwi perhaps you all will get to see them too. I also think that it is time for some new pictures for our profile - must keep up to date mustn't we? We

42

have some of Cat that may or may not get posted. Ok ok! Back to work I go! Defined benefit plans wait for no woman! Pesky secretaries!

07/16/2005
Ahhh! Last evening at the Taj we had fun, met some lovely new people then went home and - you guessed it - fucked like sex-starved rabbits. I was wearing my fluffy bunny disguise too. Notice the ears?!? Well, to day is the day for housework, blackening the driveway once again, fixing the exhaust on the Expedition, and some more whacking of the shrubberies. I may even go so far as to vacuum!! Yes, I do know what that machine is for - there's no need to be snippy. But, oh dear! It looks like rain! Well, certain things will just have to wait for next Saturday then. Hurray! Did the laundry already. I try to get as much done before Cat returns from work because I certainly will not get anything done once he is back! BTW the only jokes I know are very bad ones - so don't ask. He's back! Early! No, no! I haven't changed the sheets yet! Heeeeellllppp!!!

07/17/2005
For hilarity one cannot beat the Monty Python and the Holy Grail movie. Simply is just not possible. Next come the Jeeves and Wooster films. My daughter does a great Aunt Agatha! These movies set out to be funny, of course. The incidental humor is often the best however. Such as when the tool acquisitive American male looking at the Sears Craftsman flyer and his son taps his feet together and intones "There's no place like Sears...there's no place like Sears." Or hanging upside down in the inadvertently inverted automobile by one's seatbelts

saying "Hubby will not be pleased." Ya think?!?!? My hydrangea are looking lovely this year btw. Such a blue! Marvelous! Perhaps I will show them to Cat once he recovers from last night? Perhaps I will show him something else. One never knows with me.

07/18/2005

Sorry but I am too focused on extracting the very last ounce of pleasure out of all of those delicious big furry men to be at all bi - yes this is the lady speaking (as always). CELL PHONE USERS - just dial 911. The police have those computers in their cars and will look you up. Lets see what else was being spoken of...oh yes! Long toe nails! Not into feet. *waves a hand brushing away the topic* Sorry but I have been pulling boxes out of the store rooms finding items for my daughter to take with her. Microwave, TV, stereo, innumerable coffee mugs, old drapes - you know the sort of thing. Sofa, Rugs. Dried flowers. I am not saying that my store rooms are a cornucopia of delights but there's some useful stuff in there. If only I could find it! I wonder what's in this box?

07/19/2005

"Vaginas are adaptable depending upon the arousal and internal musculature of the lady involved so NO, penis size is not that important unless it is invisible to the naked eye or about the same size as the lady's smallest finger whereupon it just gets embarrassing with everyone standing around wondering what to say. Those with serious appendages are limited in what activities they will be permitted to participate in. So Gentlemen, overall having say 5 to 9 operational inches is your

44

best bet with thicker being better than thinner since you evoke neither fear nor pity and you have more options as to employment." Aunt Agatha's Answers, pg 371

OMG the daughter is up and out of bed before noon!?!?! As soon as I am within reach of the sofa, I will faint! No, not really but she found it amusing. It is amazing the amount of stuff she is permitting me to palm off onto her! Very nice! One can enter my main store room and breathe now as there's actual air space! Once the son graduates and gets his apartment, I might even be without stores completely! Then we will move without leaving a forwarding address and enter the Parents Protection Program! Well, it is a thought and yes, my kids do think I am silly, cute and adorable. It comes from teaching them to stay by me in the supermarket by intimating that if they blinked I'd be off like a shot - ESCAPE! "Mother. You're not getting away THAT easily. If you aren't careful, there will be no bookstore for you!" Darn! Oh, and Cat's in trouble. He shall have to do some serious groveling and/or appeasement to get out of this one!

07/20/2005
Well, well, well; Cat does not know where and how he erred! This will hurt. And YES I am a raging sex machine rampaging over the landscape, tyvm. And all of that energetic desire is going to be focused upon Cat! Bwahahahahaa!

The polo season is half over! This causes me great distress. Getting out into the country, albeit manicured, and in the company of horses and horse-people is always both relaxing and refreshing. I like hearing my exhaust reverberate off the concrete as much as the next person but there comes a time when one simply has to lie on the grass and watch the clouds roll on by. This point is reached when the old slogan 'reach out and touch someone' begins to mean strangulation. Everyone has their favorite method; my son, for example, prefers defenestration while my daughter favors that ice cold glance that rips the flesh from your bones. (Can't think where she got that from!)

I will now pay bills! *drawing a small circle on the floor, standing in the center of said circle holding envelopes, tossing envelopes above head, paying all of those that landed inside the circle* There! That's done!

07/21/2005
And the groveling went quite well last night *EG* Some of the new pictures have made it up onto our profile. B&W experimentals but hey! we are going through a phase. Wanna watch? *w* If so, you'll have to get with Cat.

Have you ever read Desmond Morris? If so, you would have learned that the attraction for women with flat tummies and tight skinny waists is because it means she isn't pregnant and you are therefore 'in with a chance'? Wide hips and pronounced breasts indicate ease with child bearing and sustaining. Even showed, in the PBS program, a group of ladies getting ready for a night on the town by padding up their hips then covering it all with these huge dresses. "hips through which a child will enter the world with consummate ease" is how he narrated this sequence. LOL If you watch people getting

46

ready to go out 'mate catching', you can tell what is important in that society. Interesting. So what does this say about the recent blog entries on breasts? Y'all hungry?

The retirement housing development for swingers sounds very nice! Each house should have a large room capable of holding four king sized beds and with one wall as the screen for the projector which would be a tv as well as video thing. Imagine having a home theatre link up with your house party. Surround sound anyone?

Off to polo ,fingers crossed in hope, tomorrow followed by the TAJ!! Then a party on Saturday - perhaps I should rest up?

07/22/2005
Ah! To befriend or not to befriend - before engaging in wild rampant skin on skin full body contact SEX. There is a lot to be said for laughing as you roll around on the bed but either way will work. At least in this lifestyle (LOL) I do not have to remember if Harold's hiding under the bed and George is in the closet - or is it vice versa - and your wife meeting your girlfriend doesn't immediately lead to WW3. Polyamorous R Us!

I hope, I hope, I hope, I hope - that there will be polo tonight! The ground has been too wet for it these past few weeks and I am slowly going crazy!!! Once I've gone beyond my favorite prescription (take two men and call me in the morning) you know it is bad. Then it will be on to the (kisses are free btw) Taj to meet people who just might want to indulge in silken dalliance with us. I will bring some music this time - see if you guess which songs are from my collection.

So which would you prefer guys - the kitten or the tigress? The first five answers win a prize.

07/24/2005
Wonderful day today - doing stuff and things around the house and then a MARVELOUS party tonight! Yes!!! Did not come even near my 'limit' but, hey! we had a one hell of a good time! HAPPY BIRTHDAY WAYNE! and yes I did get a small nip in *eg* I then tucked Cat into bed and will shortly join him there - the poor guy's been working far too hard lately. So Sunday will be a quiet and relaxed day around the house. Just chillin' as the kids would say.

So, the average American woman is a size 12/14 huh? Well, I am a size 16 with a bit of extra but nothing too shocking and I have these legs - as some of you can attest - and a delight in sex. Love it! On that note may I remind you fellows to come to me with joy in your heart and fire in your eye. A light touch may delight some others but I want more! There's nothing like masculine ardor to get my twin V-12s singing! Don't hold back for with me its more "gentlemen, defends yourselves" than anything. LET THE PLAY BEGIN

07/25/2005
Well, bad news has come our way. Seems brother-in-law hasn't eaten since last Wed and all major systems shutting down and it may not be long now. Not entirely unexpected as he's been battling cancer for 10 years. Unlike us, he's never done anything to

bring it on - twas just the hand he was dealt. The Reaper has had him by the ankles, pulling him into the grave but he had been digging his fingers into the earth, you know, putting up a fight - guess he's just lost his grip. Check your ankles for fingerprints daily, my friends, and get out there and LIVE!

07/26/2005
Everyone run out into the street and yell "Be reasonable!" Am I that controlling? Hmmmm. I tried an experimental squeak (refer to someone's blog) but it only drew the cat. And not the Cat neither. *sigh* Today is supposed to be a scorcher so today's the perfect day to get my MGB inspected!! I shall wear my skimpy bathing suit too. Take lawn chair and a book so whilst the inspector is working...I won't be.

Thank you for your kind notes re brother-in-law. Called last evening and it seems that the family is gathering. The question seems to be how do we support my 80 yr old father-in-law who doesn't want to know? Surround him with grandkids? Thus far he has 6 of them ranging from 23 years to 5 months and they do make an impressive crew. It might help.

Time to study up on the Tax Consequences of Executive Benefits. I am almost done with Course 4. One more course and then it is the certification exam in November. What have I signed myself up for? Eeeeeeeeeeeek!

07/27/2005
My daughter has snitched my cordless phone again - the one with the office line on it. Well, that just

means they will wake her up. Woman spends half the night chatting with her beau and then expects to sleep the morning away. HAH! Not how it works, dear! Next time take one of the cordless house phones with you! Silliness!

Writing the client newsletter, re-vamping brochures, and updating website. Soon have to update From ADV Parts I and II due in Sept. Have to run all of it by my lawyers first. So am already late! Once more into the breech! *starting spellcheck* Did I write that?!?! OMG! Send me back to school!

And I am eagerly looking forward to my mini-vacation this weekend!!! Hopefully my fried will come through with a place to stay. Ocean City, Maryland most likely doesn't have a spare room anywhere and sleeping in the truck would not be my first choice. Oh well! May the Devil Take the Hindmost!

07/28/2005
Pesky males! How is it that every time you have something heavy to carry or lift, there isn't a hulking male weightlifter around to carry or lift it for you? Instead I have a 70 year old mommy with CHF and me and one bright orange shopping cart from Home Depot. Is one bucket of coal tar worth this effort?

Watching my mom and daughter in the kitchen attempting to mix, sift and scald ground walnuts in milk while reading the recipe and get in eachother's way and squabbling good-naturedly is HILARIOUS! They are making Slovenian Nut Roll in a kitchen that is 'too small for the both of us'. And then hubby gets in there and starts putting utensils into the dishwasher. "I was using that! " OMG too funny for words!

The weekend is almost here!! That means the trip to OC MD is close! So I am washing and packing up my small train case and getting ready. Did my hair and shaved - no, NOT there - and double checking to make sure that the toys are there. Almost forgot the iPod! Some $$, some gasoline, the cell phone recharger. The wine, the brie and the crackers. It is amazing the amount of stuff I feel is necessary for a weekend! Betcha Cat just gets by with just a razor and a toothbrush!

AUGUST
2005

08/01/2005

And life continues! Our weekend at OC MD was highlighted by rain, cloudiness, and showers! The water and the air were equally wet. Fortunately I was able to brighten my outlook by spending a great deal of time within the circle of Cat's arms! Purrrrr! We did get to meet one couple from apg the first night there and then visited Seacrets upon their recommendation but it wasn't an apg weekend. Nice to get out of town and have both time and energy for eachother. Ahhhhhhhhh! So now it is back to the grindstone!

08/02/2005

It must be a rule tucked away somewhere in the fine print that whoever is interested in you is one million and three-quarter miles away from you while those who live next door do not want you on a silver platter with , or without, that apple in your jaws. Which would be okay except I have no time and enough conflicts in my schedule for this month that it wouldn't help if I were cloned several times over each very fetchingly attired. I am not stressing. I am not stressing. I am not stressing. LOL

Of course, people indulge in fabrication!! Look at your income tax return! We all lie almost all of the time to anyone who might even possibly be listening. Take literally that warning flag that women wave in front of their erring husbands "FINE". That is a lie because, as every male over the age of 3 years knows, fine is precisely what the situation is not. And the male statement of "yes, dear" does not mean he agrees with you and vice versa. The question then becomes is a lie in fact a lie if everyone knows it is false?

Well, it is time to decide if I change the paint color in the daughter's old room or not. She moved out yesterday - very sad. But expected. So do I keep it periwinkle or do I not? Hmmmm. Curtains and carpeting is a straw-beige, and the trim is white.

08/03/2005

What to show in pix is whatever you want to show and whatever you feel comfortable showing. But I must admit that even I have trouble asking the guys in the bar to drop their pants so I can recognize them from their posted photos! I do wish you guys would stop being so shy! All too often the only pix visible are of the female of the pair and while this might be something that interests Cat - it does nothing for me. Come on, guys! Give me something willya? Take off your shirt, perhaps?

Was a stressful day and I don't want to talk about it! But at least Cat was there for me! Hmmmm. Very snuggleable is Cat. The perfect refuge after a rough day, a cloudy day, in fact any day!

Tomorrow is a house day - fixing up stuff and tidying – very, very dull. Irritating because it will just need to be done all over again in a little while. Sorry to be such a drag. Ok, ok It will look great!

08/04/2005

Well, I did not get as much done as I had hoped to but what has been done is very good so I did good today. We shall have a picnic dinner in front of the television watching a romantic comedy together curled up on the sofa. Yes, the same sofa. I told you

Cat was infinitely snuggleable. So tonight we will snuggle!

Some groceries followed me home but while my Expedition (named Ganesh for obvious reasons) yes we name our autos, was lounging in the parking lot some fool bumped it and left a bit of paint, a dent, and a slightly pushed back bumper on the left front corner. Man, I hate that! And, of course, whoever it was did not leave a note. I hate that too btw. And I had dropped something on my foot in the store so was unhappy to begin with. Note to self: stop juggling items off the shelves.

There had better be polo tomorrow (forecasting T-storms again) and the TAJ had better be SWINGING because I surely do need them both! On a lighter note - why is it that the notice "no user serviceable parts inside" act like a beacon to some people? Mind you, I think it is cute as all get out, but it does seem to be somewhat "I'm doing this because I shouldn't" don't you think?

08/05/2005
Once again we have too many places to go and things to do tonight! Wheeeeeeeeeeee. So look for us careening through the landscape as we try to get to all of them! Do not linger in the left hand lane tonight, folks! Cat will have to drive since I have to change in the truck. Can I wear red pumps with a coral dress? Or should I just stick with the orange sandals? It is Beach/Pool party night so I will be wearing my bright orange thong bikini too. This could get wild. *eg* Gentlemen: defend yourselves!!

Ganesh is a white Ford Expedition; Jeeves is the maroon MGB, Baby is the maroon and gray HD WideGlide, Big Boy is the ruby red HD Classic Ultra Glide, and FyrTygr is the white Ford F150. The odd blue Jeep CJ we are restoring is named AngelKitten which is too long for a license plate but oh well. The white Honda scooter car and the blue Tahoe are still awaiting their names. Just so you know.

Standard polo fare: well it used to be tuna fish salad sandwiches and beer but we have evolved to Carr's crackers, Brie and red wine. Someone else brought Virginia baked ham, a whole ham mind you, and corn bread. And Grace made jambalaya and brought fresh fruit. Several roasted chickens appeared out of nowhere along with several bottles of white wine. This all raises the question of are we going to watch the games or are we going for the food? I may have to begin exercising!!!

08/07/2005
We managed to hit two out of three engagements yesterday evening - polo was canx due to T-Storms - the M&G went fairly well, another bi-woman kiss for me *sigh*- and the Taj was GREAT!! Lots of men!!

I agree - please say 'no thank you very much' or 'not if you were the last couple on earth' or even 'drop dead' - just say something! I think we will erase our wishlist and start over. Please note - those on our wishlist are usually closer to us but alas! it seems these are the ones who aren't interested in us. The Rule seems to be working.

56

Just spent 4 hrs going out to BWI, circumnavigating the terminal for 1 hour, and then driving back - having picked up my quarry - please use Dulles next time! Either that our get a cell phone that works. Pretty please! Why do people insist upon darting out into the left most lane in front of me without looking? Can they not see this huge white beast barreling down upon them, flashing its headlights? Then there are those who linger in the left lane, also in front of me, when they aren't passing anyone. I especially enjoy it when they are talking swaying from side to side in the lane and talking on their cell phones, and yes they are in front of me once again.

We will be painting the daughter's old room, periwinkle with white trim with iron furniture and using it as a spare bedroom. As the second spare bedroom to be precise. The other one is orange with white trim and blonde oak furniture - looks very nice.

08/08/2005
How did this happen? Excuse me, I feel faint. I have to sit down. That's better! How did we end up with an entire week with no apg engagements?!?! I shall have to have a word with our Social Department. We simply cannot have this! It is unfortunate but the only playtime we have available this month (August) is during the week. Let us review: 6th pick up Mom from BWI, 13th get son from college (PSU), 20th party at Mom's house for the family and the 27th the Silk n Skin. I have a new outfit for that - you will have to see it! So you see, no time unless its during the week.

Periwinkle, periwinkle, periwinkle! It is not that I mind painting - I just dislike wearing the stuff as well! On the wall, girl! Get it on the wall! Don't step into the roller tray of paint either! Careful! *sigh* I hope this stuff comes off. I look like I was playing paintball without the gear! Perhaps if I bathed in gasoline? Love the smell of refined petroleum products!

Sad to see so many upset by appearances. Why waste your time worrying about the outside of persons when the insides are so much more intriguing, fun and delicious? Look, if they don't float your boat, they don't float your boat - but there's no need to make a philosophy about it! Are you sure you aren't vanilla?

08/09/2005
Having been a bad, bad kitty, I shall now be sweet and lovable. *a sly look* "Patience, my dear, patience" is what I am being told. I have not been blessed with vast amounts of the stuff so if you see claw marks on the table legs, please do not be surprised. We are speaking figuratively, of course.

And I quote: "How deplorably untidy it all is! I have borrowed the cottage of a friend, and I may not unfairly plead that some part of the guilt is his. This chair - allow me to remove the eggs - is not at all uncomfortable. Somewhere" - he looked round vaguely - "there are cigarettes. Virginian, I fear." end quote. Innes, The Secret Vanguard, pg 198

Why are we here? We are here to interact both socially and sexually with as many people as will conveniently fit upon the bed. Let's see...what else

58

is in the blogs lately? Oh, yes! Single men! We do not mind single men but we haven't found just the right one yet. We haven't found the right single woman either for that matter. We shall continue looking however! So keep those postcards and letters coming!

08/10/2005

Ever notice how work interferes with a decent sex life? Either it takes up your time or it stresses you out too much. Why can't they just mail the check to the house and not require you showing up and/or actually doing anything? Sing along with me "I don't want to go to work." LOL Shame I have such a dedicated secretary keeping me to my grindstone. But if he blinks, whoosh! I am gone, baby!

My dress has arrived and as soon as Cat recovers we shall have fun opening the box and fitting me into it! Black brocade! Should look killer I tell you. Most likely will post a picture so you can see it. Those who attend THOSE parties will get to see it close up and in real life. I might wear my hair up. What do you think? Hmmm?

The daughter's old room is now freshly painted periwinkle. And so are my painting clothes. The elastic has gone out of the waistband and spent half of the time pulling my pants up. It is hard for some men to paint and laugh that hard simultaneously. Nothing lasts any more! That outfit is only 10 years old!

08/11/2005

Football?!?! On no! Not again!! LOL Sorry, lovers, but not my sport. Esp since there is no chance of me ever actually participating in it. Rally driving, anything to do with horses and - my favorite sport of all! - sex; now those I can get into!

The dress is fantastic and I look great in it, see the pix, but it is a little warm. Should be great for Halloween as well as for THOSE parties although it does take a while to get laced up into it. Cat had fun playing with my strings *w*! We took some pix for you. After careful testing, i have decided that my hair down is better than my hair up.

Other than this, there is not much to report which is a shame as we are such fun! Painted on the second coat of periwinkle, doing some business, worrying about the kids and my truck Ganesh who is making some odd sound - life is continuing as per usual. Well, time to turn on the fishes!

08/12/2005
Being camera shy and having 'control issues' - no we do not re-post pix - it is hard enough trying to get them in the first place! What you see is more or less what we have. We do not re-cycle our blogs either as I have far too much to say to do that. For example: shy men are the absolute devil! You have to calm them down AND get them excited at the same time! THEN you have reassure them that it was marvelous, great, etc., etc., etc. Hey guys, if I flush an attractive shade of pink - you've gotten it!

I may have spoken of this before but the deathwatch we have been keeping on my brother-in-law is over. He died yesterday at the ripe old age of 43 years from cancer he was unable to defeat although he put up a good fight for more than 10 years. May the

Good Lord bless and keep him. The point being live your life! It is the only one you have and it is far too short.

So you can see why we need a relaxing time of it tonight with some polo and then a few drinks with friends in the Fairfax or nearby areas. Drop us a line or two or give us a call if you have our numbers. I will be online until approx 3pm and on my cell after 5pm.

08/15/2005

Well, that was the weekend from Hell! Saturday from 6:30 am until Midnight driving, driving, DRIVING!!! What should have taken a mere 8 hours took FOREVER. A truck, for whatever reason, took out a bridge, and hundreds of cars had to go around and over the mountains via the back of beyond. A 50 mile detour to skip over a 2 mile stretch of highway. This was of course after the obligatory 2 hour traffic jam in the heat. At least this is the last time I have to take this particular trip.

We spent Sunday recovering, discussing ways and means, and playing loud music while the drinks caught up with us, nabbed us and deftly tied us up.

Things to do; things to do - so I guess I had better get on with getting them done though chatting with you all is much more fun. But my secretary is gnawing my ankle and waving papers at me. Eeeeek!

08/16/2005

No,no,no! I will not send out my guest list gangbang, or not. I refuse and I will wave my <u>Miss</u>

Manner's Guide to Excruciatingly Correct Behavior
at you if you persist! You come, and cum, because
you wish to party and because you know I only
invite cool people anyway. Do not make me stamp
my paw!

Today began with being stood up, followed by a
nice lunch with a nice man and ended with a
complete cancellation! Me, oh, my! This vetting is
becoming very hard work. Now tis Cat's turn. Let us
see if he has any better luck! I broke a claw!

I did get to take the MGB out and it was
WONDERFUL! I love hearing it reverberating off
the concrete buildings in DC! It sounds like a
Lambo! Wheeeeeeeeee! Of course, if anyone would
care to give me a Lambo I wouldn't say no but I am
not spending that on a car. So my next one is going
to be the LR3 in gold or white with all of the bells
and whistles.

08/17/2005
Yes it is different, because these are people you are
dealing with and what may have been bad for you
may not be bad for someone else. So tis best to err
on the side of being gracious and giving even the
poor performers the benefit of the doubt.

There is also a difference between fantasy play and
role-playing. Fantasy play is more unbridled and
there's no scripting. You have to be more careful
too. There was a question asked.

Well back to the grind!! See you lovely people
later!!

08/18/2005

Flying off the backswing wheeeeeeeeeeeeeee!!! Good thing I don't read these things! I have been ripping cds -using my 23 yr old son's collection of music. Is that what they call this stuff?!?!?! You have anything even remotely lyrical? OK, OK there's some good stuff. The rest sounds more like a train wreck - literally!

Tried a new scotch last night, only thing in the cabinet - go figure, Virginia Gentleman , very sweet for a scotch with a bit of honey in it somewhere - not bad. Not very smokey at all. Bourbon in a way. Will have to get some more to try as well as my favorite Laphroaig.

So lunch is off - okay but second chances are few and far between given my schedule. Family party this Saturday then another next Saturday then one of THOSE parties, you know the kind, after that during the week. Clients, polo games, evenings at the Taj meeting persons who just might be persuaded *eg*, the normal running of life - you know how it gets. Yes, yes I am coming give me a minute to finish this!

08/19/2005

Loved the lemonade stand story! Very nice of you! Now as to this 'hanging onto youth' - what are you? a vampire? Come on! I am having more fun now than ever before and I prefer men close to my own age. Give me experience!! We will see who blows who's mind first! Yeeehaw! It is all about finding those who are 'up to your weight' or if you prefer a different expression 'in your league'. I fear nothing not even aging. Haven't I said it before? Tis the person not the packaging. So shine forth and damn the wrinkles and gray hairs!!!

May the Devil Take the Hindmost!!!

and he can take the housework too! Office work, followed by housework is a bit much! As soon as I find that credit card that has no limit and no pay back, I'm hiring people to do it for me. And then I 'll get a new wardrobe. A nice brand new car. What else? Hmmm. AH, if only wishes were horses!

08/21/2005
Okay, finished the housework in a flash to drive 2 hrs to family party - which was very nice - celebrated two birthdays, two wedding anniversaries and son's graduation all at once - then skipped out and drove back another 2hrs to get home so could go to polo with the neighbors - I owe them - who then canx at the last minute and left me all alone!!! Neither gf nor bf would come with me either. What is wrong with this picture? Excuse me *sniff* I need a handkerchief. *sniff, sniff*

Would not have made the girls give the money back. Haven't any fantasies left - have done them all so no longer fantasies, and why not a gangbang? They are fun! Just because the men run rapidly in the opposite direction screaming "No, no, not again! Get away from me you horrible woman!" and I have to drag them into bed is no reason not to like them. Is it?

Went gawking at almost million dollar homes to see their justification for such a price. Nice, but their finishing work, needs work. Propane? Eeeek! That won't do. But the house was nice in spite of not having anywhere near enough land. I liked the hardwood floors, the solarium, and the extra ceiling height (10ft) but no built in shelves in the office and no cable were design misses. Balconies are only allowable if you can actually use them. They also did not use the area under the elevated deck. Plenty of orgy space in the finished basement however which had a full bath, a bar, and a home theatre room as well as several other rooms large enough for beds. Hmmm wonder where my mind's at. *w*

08/22/2005

Bet that's the last time she reports doing a good deed! Chin up, girl - at least I think you did right! Speaking of doing right - lost my sexcretary last night. He was hired away after having been in intense negotiations with me for several months. Drat! And he was perfect for the job! Apparently the commute as too much for him. Now I have to hire someone else. *pouting* All of that work! Anyone know of an alternative IT capable sexcretary/office manager? Well, my ex sexcretary is doing the right thing by being an on call consultant and helping me hire and vet a replacement. Thank you!

This also means that my office is a mess and that I will have to clean it up. I have been avoiding it for months too. Being in between contracts and hence in between sexcretaries is no fun. Seems I need someone to keep me to my wheel. A major character flaw, yes, I know but we all have at least one.

Well it is time for me to go and get prepared for this interview. We have some free time this week during the evenings excepting Tues and Thurs so get in touch with us if interested in some mind-blowing sexual adventures. I may not have any fantasies left but you might *w*. Nothing but love for ya!

08/23/2005

My turn to vent and no you cannot stop me so it is no use busting in line like that! Back of the line, buddy! Today some idiot male in a dually decided I was his dream girl of the highway. He sat next to me with his window down and his hand gesturing up and down (you know the gesture guys) whilst yelling ribald suggestions at me. I am an experienced woman but, dammit, I take my driving seriously and 70 mph on Interstate 95 is NOT the time to be trying to pick me up! The MGB is small so I could slip away from him but he kept coming back. Only the marines at the gate to Quantico stopped his pursuit. Good thing I was unarmed.

Other than that, twas a good day meeting interesting people and filling out government forms. Hey, you have your idea of fun and I have mine. Several names for the sexcretary position have been suggested and I have had two volunteers - one from apg - if only he was serious! But he said he doesn't do Windows! Drat!

The painting continues! Today it was the linen closet! Hmmmm. Needs a second coat. Bright white, of course. No sense putting a color in there. There's a work stoppage! We have run out of paint! Oh, no! And in spite of our habit of flinging paint about we managed to NOT get paint on the carpet. HURRAY!!!

08/24/2005

An other than Harley motorcycle?!?! For shame! Okay okay, we will let you in but just this once and you have buy the beer! If you offer enough, maybe hubby will part with his old one. Then again, maybe not. Hard to say - you know how attached guys become to their toys.

The work stoppage is over! Fresh paint has been delivered and is now being vigorously flung all over the linen closet. Mind the carpeting!!

Okay he says that he will do Windows and that the commute is nothing for him. The only question remaining is - is he cute enough to be a sexcretary? Hmmmm? Can he file naked without catching something important in the drawer? These are important issues here! Stop laughing!!

08/25/2005

The care and feeding, yes you have to feed them, of young males from ages 12 through 24 has tapped me out! Where does he put it all?!?! Hey come on! You are supposed to store groceries in the pantry not inside of you! Leave something for the rest of us! STOP!!! *image of woman back to refrigerator defending it* Don't you have any friends whose parents will feed you?

Up coming events include the Silk & Skin, The Warrenton Horse Show and a lovely day at the beach! Have also found fly fishing and drive a NASCAR race car as small trips/gifts to entertain two of my favorites males. BTW polo season is almost over! So we will have to find another out let - ah! - the fall point to points! HURRAY!!

I now have 4 persons wishing to be my sexcretary - I do hope they know that this means they are forever non-participatory, well, at least for as long as they are employed by me. We will see how this all works out - should be all over, except the actual work, by the first of October. The office Halloween Party should be veerrryyy interesting!

08/26/2005
Almost forgot to mention The Washington International Horse Show! I go for the Puissance. Love those big fences! If the gas prices ever decrease, I will talk about my driving very quickly in the back of beyond done for fun, but til then, horses and interpersonal communication is what you're getting.

Happy Anniversary to us! 28 years and still going strong! YES!! It can be done!

Of course it may be because we are both very stubborn people who refuse to admit to making mistakes...what me? I never!...or it may be attributed to us both having a lively sense of humor, an appreciation of the frailties of humans, and the view we both share that life is one hell of a good party! What are you waiting for?

08/27/2005

Hey! Even if his equipment isn't quite ready, a man always has his hands and mouth! With the things I can do to him (very evil grin) he will usually 'cooperate'. A little kindness and there ya go.

And yet another profile specifying a bi female in a couple. Grrrrrrrrrrrr. If I weren't such a 'demoness', I would become depressed. Okay ladies! Off you gals go - leave your husbands to my tender mercies! My latest fantasy - if we are still recording them here, is to have three men begin licking at my ankles, while I am standing, and slowly work their way upwards! You know how that will end! Give me more examples of muscles, fur, skill, and enthusiasm! Come to think of it, there's a party tonight! *w*

It is time to go and severely restrain the ivy again. I shall cut it back with extreme malice aforethought. Gardening, the way I do it, is good exercise. Kamikazi gardening!!!!!

08/28/2005

Great party last night! Nice to see a whole room of naked men! And, yes condoms are now required dress - thought everyone knew. If you require a certain variety, have them on hand perhaps in a lovely bowl on the mantle over the fireplace? Considering the variety they come in - it is nice to see manufacturers doing all they can to increase a woman's pleasure while still trying to do their best for the men.

I have to report an injury. Last night, whilst trying to slide off of the bed, I caught my shin on the wood and fell over the bench they had placed at the bed's foot. I am feeling a bit battered because of this. Please consider the ease of exit when setting up your furniture. Thank you. This has been a public service announcement from Injured Kittens Anonymous.

Well this will not get the vacuuming done! *sigh* There's always something, isn't there. Anyway will catch you all later. I have a net! And no I am not mean - you're just a sissy!

08/29/2005
A rather poor day to begin with but met a good friend for a drink and it improved tremendously! Thank you, sweety! So now for a cozy night at home within the arms of my beloved! C y'all later! *w*

08/30/2005
To Blog or not to blog, that is the question! Whether it is nobler in the minds of men to endure the absurdities of this world in silence or to electronically write about it perchance to elicit a spark in the minds of others.
I am a professional - please do not try to replicate the above at home. NEW - FINISH THE QUOTE "Those whom the gods love................."

08/31/2005
Plautus, 3rd century BCE but he was merely repeating an idea from the Greeks. Nevermind, no one's reading any of this anyway.

SEPTEMBER
2005

09/01/2005

I found it interesting that a man in Kansas City, Kansas (Tornado Alley) griped about his tax dollars going to help those "idiots who bought a house in Florida." Betcha he lives in a trailer park. Those that have the resources left, what we are seeing are those who do not have the resources and this is why we help however we can. Relatives should open their homes and hearts even to the point of driving down to get them. Unfortunately I have not been able to get in contact with mine. One family lives just 20 miles west of New Orleans; the other lives on an island off the coast of Florida. Katrina was a Category 5 hurricane people - they do not come any bigger than that. Mercy and grace upon us all but esp for all of those afflicted.

09/02/2005

Well, I tried to donate blood but ALAS the FDA has ruled that I may not. Military shots and overseas travel has made it impossible. People, if you can - please do so.

The polo season is winding down - only a few games left in our area. The Warrenton Horse Show is this weekend and the cost is a mere $5 each. We will be there for the Foxhunter events this Sunday. After this there are the fall point-to-points, the Washington International Horse Show and the Gold Cup Races.

Other than this, life continues - may be I will get my desk cleared? Still taking résumé's for the sexcretary position!

Interesting point of view in the paper today re: contraception leading to all of the usual societal ills such as divorce, marital infidelity, abortion and both spousal and child abuse. I must admit that I fail to understand their reasoning since such ills existed long before contraception came about. The only thing I can think of that contraception has done is to permit women to enjoy themselves in a sexual manner as men have done for quite some time now. The playing field has been leveled. And this is a bad thing?

On a lighter note, we have recently met some very nice people and they will be joining us at the Taj tonight. I hope to introduce them around to everyone's mutual pleasure! See you there!

Busy weekend this weekend! In fact every weekend in Sept has been filled with fun things to do! So if you aren't doing anything during the week - call us!

09/03/2005
WOW what a great time we had last night at the Taj! Sparks galore! Others had also brought in new friends so the possibilities are increasing nicely! And now.................onto the housework. Well, it must be done!

09/04/2005
The results of last night's polo match: England versus the US. England won 14 to 13 . A hard fought game and the US scored a two point goal in the final 11 seconds of the 4th chukkar. Very exciting!! Since my team lost, I had to buy the ice cream.

Saw the Ladies Sidesaddle Over Fences and the Junior Foxhunters classes at the Warrenton Horse Show! Fun but their scoring left me mystified. Some excellent horses and some superb riders - but very few were paired up that way! LOL

09/07/2005

Lets see, lounged about on Labor Day at home and then killed the closest alligator Tuesday - yes, not a bad start to the week! Someone mentioned a possible party this weekend? Hmmm? And Sunday it is Cat's birthday! Hurray! I will not longer have a toy boy (for several months at least). I have set him up with a fly fishing lesson that morning.

Did you know that you can drive a NASCAR race car in Manassas? For $300 you get 15 laps as fast as you care to go and then the racer drives you for another 5 laps as fast as he can go. Exciting! But that's the Sunday after next. *w*

Well time for me to put some clothes on - yes, I know, such a bore - but they won't let me out of the house without them! Today I shall wear all black - and no, NOT like they do it in Baghdad - with my stilettos. Attending a seminar today so have to out glam the big dogs. Ciao, darlings!!!!

09/08/2005

We are trying to, hun, we are trying! But we are only one couple! And there are so very many of you out there and only so many hours in a day.

Advance planning something for the middle of the week in the middle of October – yeah, yeah - a school night but not all of us have little tiny children anymore but great hulking galoots of returned from college kids seeking employment and their own apartments. Shoo ya pesky galoot! Don't you have an interviewer to go and annoy? You're not going to wear that tie are you?

Almost Cat's birthday! Here's hoping that my excitement helps ease his depression over and yet another year gone by! Nevermind darling! I still love ya!.... _Ciao, babies!

09/09/2005
Well, well, well! Seems someone does like my galoot! He got a call back! Now for the haircut, the cleaning of the suit and - you aren't still going to wear that tie are you? And no sneakers, sweety. Yes it is hard finding size 16 dress shoes but you have to get out there and hunt, silly kid! This is what comes from sprinkling Miracle Grow (tm) on their food when a child. You get these huge galoots.

I am fixing a feast for polo today - ham, salmon, wine, brie, crackers, tuna and one other herbed cheese - that should do it dontcha think? Maybe some breads too? How about two kinds of wine? Hmmmm.

I have found my sexcretary! The letters - good and bad - go out today so - you will know shortly if its you. Thank you for your interest, applications, and résumé's! I appreciate it! Depending upon the scope of the work I may also need a Para-planner. We shall see. Ciao, babies!

09/10/2005

Come on - the music wasn't that good. May we have something written/composed in this century please? Or perhaps from top line groups such as The Rolling Stones, Clapton and not some niche group whose name no one knows? When you think back to the 70's and 80's there were a lot of great bands but, no, all you hear are those same tired, over-played tunes! Sally getting saddle sores from riding all of that time, the guy in pickup truck gigging frogs on a date, and the two 'let's all dance as a group' ala exercise class songs - all played pretty much about the same time during the evening. Well, that helps since it is our signal to leave. Let's try Poe's Amazed instead for all of you slow dancers out there! Then perhaps something with a bit of both muscle and life to it - even humor as in Aerosmith's music. Better that than my other alternative - mug the DJ and change all of his cds!

Housework never ends! Fortunately I have one husband and one galoot to help get it all done whilst I work my fingers to the bone on this blog *eg*. Polyandry should be permitted! But then you get more in-laws - there's a drawback to everything isn't there? The cars are washed, the grass mown, the bushes trimmed and all of the weeding's done, beds changed and laundry started. Now for the vacuuming and dusting! It is now Saturday at 12:22pm. Cat's b'day party will begin soon *eg*. I have to be prepared you know. Hot tub's good even if a trifle warmer than Cat would like. I have to do my claws too. Work, work, work! LOL

We have too much stuff in this house! Perhaps we should hold an apg group garage sale? What do you think? It might be interesting.

09/11/2005
No, I cannot say that hanging out with my vanilla friends has become a bore - there's always something to talk about and to laugh about. But then, they expect me to be slightly wayward in any case so no harm done. Cat never has that problem being a very compartmented person.

Polo was a round robin tournament this past week with three teams playing two chukkars each in a rotation. All of our selected teams lost - for shame! But we did have a good time with our feast, the people, and the absolutely wonderful weather out in the green of the country. I cannot tell you how restorative we find being out there watching people trying to ride eachother's horses and yet somehow making it off the field alive.

Indulged Cat with a small but intense birthday party *w* - just the two of us! NIN playing downstairs, lowered lights, some wine - you know what happened - again and again. So 48 'kisses' later, he's happy but exhausted. Sent him off fly fishing today to relax and recuperate. Happy Birthday, Darling!!!

09/12/2005
The fly fishing lesson went very well! Cat has discovered a new hobby and has also found that he has a knack for it! HURRAY! He had wanted me to come along but, well, when I cast someone ends up with a hook in their cheek. This is why I do not go

78

fishing. Nor do I play darts or shoot pool - if I do, someone ends up hurt. But I have other talents *s*

The polo season will end on the last Friday in September so we are checking out the dates for the Point-to-points. I will have to remember to bundle up and stay warm as the chill descends - I adore summer! For one thing I can wear my skimpy summer dresses! *eg* and my thong bikinis.

I will need some really good suits soon - anyone know where I can get about three, three piece women's suits? Jackets I can find readily but when it comes to skirts and slacks, they are always too short or cut incorrectly.

09/13/2005
Thank you for all of your hints on where to go to find suits. I am sure to looks smashing this autumn! Professionally speaking, of course. Btw, for really exquisite jackets go to Horse Country in Warrenton, VA. Expect to spend some money but you will never look better!

Remember The Shocking Blue? No? But you do remember the song "Venus" dontcha? "She's got it!" etc. How about The Troggs? They did "Wild Thing". And then there's that anthem to incoherency "Louie, Louie" by The Kingsmen. Yeah we used to know how to swing it with the latest but we've become lazy - get your kids to recommend some modern tunes to you, people and give up the gigging frogs tune! You wanna slow dance? Try Poe's "Amazed" from her album "Haunted". Thank you. This has been a public service announcement.

This Friday I shall be wearing a little black dress with high heels. I tell you this now so that you will not fall over in amazement when you see us at the Taj this Friday. Yes, I do have legs. And yes, I do know how to use them too *w*. Lets see if you can keep up.

09/14/2005
No, you should have had a plan, tested and practiced; DP without anal means oral and vaginal; and since The 10 Commandments are religious, they belong in a religious context - just as we don't have astrophysics from the pulpit so we do not have Genesis in science class in whatever guise Genesis chooses to appear this week. Fair is fair.

Just read Imam Feisal Abdul Rauf's book. Still displays a fundamental disconnect. He should read Saoud's Burned Alive for a more immediate grasp of the main issue.

Lets see...what else could cause controversy? *w* I love my SUV? I am not always PC? Bathrobes, sheets and towels should be white so you can bleach them? Think, kitten, think! There must be something that will get them mailing you with fire in their eyes!

09/15/2005
Technically, we are all the same race - homo sapiens regardless of our individual hues. How many times have I said it? Tis the person not the packaging. You do remember hearing/reading that dontcha? Of course when it come to sex - whatever floats your boat or doesn't is up to individual

determination just as in I adore furrrr and have no interest in women. Cat does but that's just him.

There's no food in this house! Cat will waste away to nothing and I wouldn't like that. Sooo, I had better get off the computer and into the supermarket. Buy gasoline first, of course, or I won't make it there and back. Oh! Get dressed BEFORE leaving the house. Yes that would be a good idea too. Keys...where are my keys? Stop thinking about Cat and get your mind out of the bed, girl!

Lord, what a day it is going to be today! Well, off to the fray! Y'all enjoy yourselves *w*

09/16/2005
Why can't we all just get along? Because you stubbornly insist upon being your own person. You continue to defy my rule! Shame on you! Now quit being silly and lay down on the bed and do what the not-so-nice lady says!

Such a depressing day - bill paying time, you see. This is why I do them on Friday. There's polo on Fridays and that will take the sting out of watching the dollars flowing in the wrong direction, that is say - away from me.

Cat is of the opinion that the 16 inch tiles will make the room look smaller than the 12 inch tiles and I disagree saying that the more unbroken the expanse, by grout lines, the larger it appears. It would be similar to wide board wooden flooring vs the strip. Yes, I know - husbands are not supposed to have

81

opinions but one does have to ask them if only just for form's sake. Let controversy prevail!

09/19/2005
Great weekend! The Taj was fun, the day at the beach was fantastic and the 15 laps around the track in a NASCAR racecar was AWESOME!! The sex was marvelous and yummy as it always is. (Oooooooooo yeah!) Sorry we couldn't make it to the party - it would have been FUN! But we hope you will keep us in mind. Cat has a hard time focusing my mind elsewhere and I tell him it's his own fault for being so attractive to me.

Oh dear! Autumn is upon us and I haven't spent nearly enough time driving my convertible, playing in my garden, and doing all of those things I love to do when it is blazing hot outside like getting my XMas shopping done in August.

Lets see, Halloween is coming up and I have a mind blowing costume ready to go and YES, it is a costume. Some people complained about my domme biker chick outfit last year saying that it wasn't a costume. *pouting* This year it is "Queen of the Night".

09/20/2005
I am uncertain whether to be chuffed or annoyed - I have been described as 'fast, loud, and dangerous'. Hmmmm. Is that good or bad? I am guessing that it depends upon the man involved. There are some men who delight in poking a tigress with a stick or tease her with a witty remark. Just wait until I get him in bed without his clothes on!

OK the decision has been made. Large 16 inch tiles will be used because there are few things more tedious than scrubbing grout with a toothbrush on your hands and knees. Now all we need is a suitable professional with fair prices, a good eye for the layout, and the ability to speak English so we can understand him/her. Work to be done in October.

So are we going Goth for Halloween this year? You know lots of black and white with red all over? Very Celtic btw. Which suits me since I am. So who's coming as the ancient goddess of war in a tattered raven outfit? We could have the Woman in White too with her diaphanous (sp) draperies wafting about her naked form. One of my favorite holidays.

09/21/2005
Doing the caged tigress bit here and cannot settle down to doing anything productive. This is one very bad week for us and the tension's only going to get worse. Friday brings news - good or ill - there' no way of telling. But if ill then all hell's going to break loose and wreck havoc over the landscape.

But enough of me going out of my mind! You haven't paid your dues to hear that!

Rita Mae Brown has come out with a new book and it is excellent! Guns, Germs and Steel remains hard to plow through but it is interesting - not quite sure if I agree with him. I am supposed to be studying but you see how it is. Reading extensively is my oldest vice. No, we will not discuss the others I have acquired since then. Although I have acquired some interesting ones.

09/22/2005

BTW have I mentioned that I also love lively debate? Some of you are discovering this. Its all good however! But its not me who's wearing that pink tutu from Walmart. Sorry, but I am too much an 'Emma Peel in her black leather catsuit' for that. Bring it on, Spicy man! *insert mischievous laughter here*

I don't mind drama because I have a nice little haven to which I can return but there is a limit. A play or a skit is okay but a grand opera is not. I usually think of the bar fight scene in Butch Cassidy and the Sundance Kid where the fight rages about them and they simply remove their beers from the table when a body hurtles into it, smashing the table while they quietly just keep drinking . Or the guy in college who set his matchbook alight in class, you could smoke in class back then, when he tried to just light the one. He simply lit his cigarette during the flare-up, blew out the matchbook and quietly placed the remnants on his desk. No problem! Often society demands a degree of poise.

Yes you do have to laugh at life even when disaster is staring you in the face. When Death smiles at you, wink back! Yeah, yeah. Now it is time to go sit on the library deck out in the sun and enjoy both my garden and a drink! Ciao, babies!

09/23/2005

I spoke too soon, apparently. The debate has been called due to the weather. It was fun while it lasted. But then, lots of things are.

84

09/24/2005

Some persons are just sooo romantic Rose petals?!?! Sorry, but they would just get in the way. We are seriously into sex. We only chat to see if we think similarly. Then its on to the seduction. Today it was marshalling the marshal of the President's Cup and tomorrow, well, we do not plan on getting much work done.

BTW the polo was great - after we drove around, got lost and a friendly man in a Suburban drove manically down an unpaved road and showed us where to turn left. Wheeee. Then Cat's truck decided that it had had enough and we lost the brakes. Oh dear! We made it back to Middleburg then to Fairfax and we had a picnic in the dining room. While Cat fulminated about his lack of stopping power. Any wonder why we were late to the Taj hmm? After the Taj there was no stopping either of us!

Apparently the debate was called due to agreement. No, no, we are beginning another! So okay its now an argument not a debate. Semantics! Gotta love 'em! Ciao babies!!

09/26/2005

Follow-up?!?!? I thought a date was a date and that only death excused you from keeping it. Our schedules are tighter than most so when we set a date - it is in concrete. So expect us to be there - even if everyone else wimps out. Now, if you wimp out, well, that's something else again esp if you are the host/hostess. Nevermind, we will find something to do *w*.

Just received a very nice email from a good looking, clean cut, single guy saying thanks for the good time - the trouble is - it wasn't us!! So Diana of the wine party in Reston - he says thank you and your hubby is an extremely fortunate man!

I am thinking of cutting my hair. What do you think? Just to a short fluffiness that's rather RB so I can look killer without having to spend hours having Cat comb the knots due to intense sexual activity out of it. One of those shake your head, dahlink, and go haircuts.

09/27/2005
Why? Because when it is your turn for disaster to strike, it is also your turn to receive help - that's why Spicy man. Else we'd have to de-populate all of the Midwest (tornadoes), California (earthquakes), and Seattle (volcano), anything remotely within reach of the volcano slumbering beneath Yellowstone which is the entire US west of the Appalachians, all of the Gulf and SE US coast (hurricanes), the entire NE US and Great Lakes (nor'easters) and everything north of Tejas due to possible ice storms and blizzards which doesn't leave a lot of living space. Mind you, those are just the threats from Mama Nature.

We shall see how my new hair turns out. I have received two votes - both from males who had to have their opinions wrenched out of them. Cat actually said that I wasn't getting an opinion out of him that easily! Perhaps we have trained men too well? But he's cool with it. The proposed hairstyle is on page 6 of the new Bloomingdale's catalog.

Otherwise life continues to hurtle its way towards disaster - we shall see how it turns out since there's two weeks left to run. You will have to excuse me now since I have to make a couple of calls. C Y'ALL

OCTOBER
2005

10/02/2005

Happy birthday you blue-haired, ball stapling, lemonade drinking freak.

10/04/2005

Have not been blogging lately - just not enough time and not in the mood to make time. Polo is over for the year. *sob* But perhaps there are other things I can do to relax. Went to a party last Saturday and it was fun!

Everyone likes, I mean REALLY likes, my new hairstyle. This Friday, I am having it colored and may even get a treat - SH may stop by the salon! No, it will NOT be dyed blue, thank you very much. Just some highlights.

It has been a decent week. Haven't wanted to strangle Cat all weekend! Imagine that! LOL But he has since made up for it so all is well. Remind me to call Frank tomorrow - okay?

Thank you, S H. Would be nice to see you, esp after reading Estate Transfers During Life. Yegods! The accumulated persiflage of lawyers is more than enough to drive one to drink. All one really needs to know in life is: when the califraction of one's livery is imminent, one absquatulates.

I called Frank but he wasn't in as he was supposed to be so I will have to call again later on. Be sure to remind me again. Thank you.

I have to go. I have an injured buddy in my hot tub. I have some box moving to do. I should pay the gas bill. Oh, yes! And I might even get some work done! Ciao, babies!!

10/05/2005
Well I got very little work done. Very saddening! 2 cancelled appts too. But I manage to renew the new HD's registration. I think the noise in the back end of the Expedition is from the wheel bearings. So that will have to go in even as the other truck, you remember the other truck's in for brakes, comes out. If it has tires or testicles..................

A word about management style. Better to enable than to disable.

Taxation of Indirect Skips. How very interesting! Those lovely people at the IRS, yes, yes, very nice people! I had better clean my glasses before I read this particular section. There's a point-to-point this weekend as well as a wine festival. Care to go, sweeties? Just mail us here! Ciao for now!

10/07/2005
Thank you for all of the kind notes from people liking my new hairstyle - tis just a bit of camouflage - who would expect such a cute fluffy bunny of having evil designs upon you big bad men? Other than Cat who keeps tousling my hair and grinning as he walks by and avoids my small attempts at retribution.

Oh, I talked to Frank. Next call is scheduled for next Friday. Let us all hope for a positive and swift outcome.

Now if you will excuse me, it is time to crank up the tunes and dance naked in the rain! Fortunately all of the neighbors are at work! Kisses where you most need them!

10/09/2005
Well the naked rain dancing did not go so well. Apparently not all of my neighbors work. Fortunately I found this out in the nick of time and was able to quickly scamper back under cover before being noticed. Stealthy Nip!

Stage 2 of the new hairstyle has been achieved if perhaps a trifle fluffier than expected but it looks great! Stage three is scheduled for the 27th at 11 am. Thanks, SH!!!! Had a great time. She's wonderful!!! The drive home wasn't all that fun but then these people cannot drive well at the best of times let alone when its raining. The first rule of driving is to get the hell out of the way!!!

Hubby's under a car so I guess I might as well get some of this paperwork off my desk, get the mail sorted and catch up on my biz mag reading. Ho hum! Perhaps I will get some boxes stored away too or does that sound too ambitious? Ciao for now!

10/11/2005
Finally, back online! I go so used to being 'connected' that being offline was a severe trauma! I may never recover! *melodramatic pose of your choice* Perhaps some specialized care from Cat will help?

Remind me to call Frank this Friday morning.

Cat will be tossed out this Friday to the Taj all alone! I will not be there. Ladies, see what you can do for him please. Nothing sadder than a man unsupervised.

10/12/2005

It happened again last night! Someone was doing 60mph in the fast lane! And reading! Yegods! So we now have to dodge in and out of the other traffic and cross multiple lanes just to get around one person who could have simply moved over for a few seconds! And they wonder why we get 'aggressive'! Nothing like increasing the danger to all of us just to spare you from having to move over for a few! You are all fortunate Lamborghini doesn't make tanks. You get two to three lanes to play in - I get one; and I quote "slower traffic keep right" Any questions?

another interim hair photo posted

Jan Neuharth wrote <u>The Hunt</u> - I highly recommend it. Oh, and Adesta Communications are spending literally millions of dollars laying buried fiber optics directly in the middle of the new southbound lanes of the newly widened Rte 15. Too funny! C ya, kids!

10/13/2005

Herpes? Yes, you can transmit even while not having an outbreak according to the NIH and CDC. No thank you very much. Get tested and always wear a condom. Ladies if allergic then supply what you can use - various sizes. The small ones are in the green bowl and those for those 'horses' out there are in the steamer trunk over there. Speaking of which...

Remind me to call Frank tomorrow. Thank you.

TV shows and sports may be fun but I think a man who knows his business is the BEST entertainment! OH WOW, what fun I have been having!! WHEEEEEEEEEEEEE! If, as it has been said, orgasm-ing three times a week is what your heart needs then mine is in fantastic shape!! So baby, darling, sweetheart, bring yourself over here and leave those clothes at the door!

10/14/2005
Frankly I do not do 'naughty schoolgirl' et al, very well. Can't we do something more for the aggressive women for a change? Can't we do a 'Toy-Boy', 'Gladiator' or 'Lifeguard' night? Ladies, drag out your fantasies and let's see what we can come up with! (keeping my fantasies firmly under wraps of course because, trust me, you don't want to know what they are; heh, heh, heh)

Yes, yes I am calling Frank! The phone's ringing!

Cat will be tossed out this Friday to the Taj all alone! I will not be there. Perhaps he will not be there. But if he is: Ladies, see what you can do for him please. Nothing sadder than a man unsuper-vised.

10/17/2005
Peter, Paul and Mary recorded the definitive Puff the Magic Dragon way back when. My Mom was, and most likely still is, a big fan of this particular

94

group. I myself prefer something more along the lines of R&R myself so please do not ask me how the songs went or what the words were - but Puff is ultimately a sad song.

Frank said to give him a call today. Great! I woke up with a sore throat - this is not the time for me to be talking I have to be better soonest! Things to do and people to meet!

Nothing much to report. Had a good if quiet weekend and kept busy. We are resting up for this weekend - three parties, yes, THOSE parties,, to attend!! FUN!!!

10/18/2005
Apparently someone does not like receiving one liners. What a shame! They we are exhorted to sell ourselves! Tell us why we should meet you! Well, that is the point of this site isn't it? You are here to perhaps NOT meet others? As the spokeswoman for this particular couple, I shall say that you will never, ever meet anyone like us - mad, bad, and exultant rejoicers that we are.

Frank wasn't there, left a message, he hasn't returned my call so must be unwell again. I shall try again tomorrow.

Spent most of yesterday in a Nyquil induced drowse and I am indeed better, thank you. A nice hot shower and I will be running on all cylinders again! Note: in case of illness or upset with Ms. Nip - just apply heat. Cat adds - make her wear her slippers!

10/19/2005

I know it is late but I have uploaded the photos taken last night. My new hair at Stage Two. Sorry I wasn't smiling but I wasn't feeling my best - a slight cold. Still not quite over it. It didn't stop me pouncing upon my photographer however, much to his delight!

10/21/2005
Had a small but GREAT party yesterday afternoon - a bit of Group Therapy - to limber up for the weekend. Tonight will be delicious as well. Then there's Saturday's house party! Pot luck and I have no idea of what to bring! Given the weather I may bring chili but that requires a permit from the Nuke people. Then there are those warning signs and specialist personnel that have to be deployed around the house so I ask myself if a pot of chili is quite worth it?

My office is actually clean and tidy!!! Amazing!!! Never thought it would happen. Neither did Cat to tell the truth, but hard labor eventually accomplishes its object. Oh, and Frank said to call him Monday at 11am so be sure to remind me.

I am not a winter person. Cold weather, changing leaf colors, snow, 'crispness' in the air - YUCK! Give me those balmy heat-laden summer dog days anytime! The only thing to enjoy about winter are the holidays (surely you know by now that I am always up for a good party?) and now we have one per month! Halloween, Thanksgiving, Christmas, New Year's and Valentine's Day! YES! All of the big ones! Heck I may even be able afford actual gifts this year!!! Now to make a list hmmmm Ciao babies!

10/22/2005

I apologize for disappointing but unable to attend party as cannot stop coughing, sneezing, and napping. I shall curl up in bed instead with my comfy clothes on and try to get better. Also gave this to Cat who then gave it back to me and you know how that goes. *yawning* sorry, another nap coming on. Ciao.

10/24/2005

Grrrrrrrrrrrr, some progress is being made but not enough!! I have begun wearing my sweat clothes and thick wooly socks. You all should thank me for staying away. Cat's lost his voice almost entirely and mine is not much better! About the best I can hope for now is to make lunch on Wednesday and my final hair appt this Thursday. There's another sex party Friday but I am not sure about attending that esp since there's a Halloween Party on Saturday; costumes optional. Poor Cat has to drag himself to work tomorrow so if you will excuse me, I'll just go and tuck him into bed now. Later!

10/25/2005

It seems I have been missing blogs written by a dear friend. Sorry, hun. And, you are welcome! I glad you are both very happy and wish you both the best! Would just like to see you more often, ya know!

Keep it up, G! Only, you do know about me and my locomotive habits don't you? Has me worried. But Thursday will come and I will be there! I hope your schedule remains open so we can meet!

More improvement! Cat can speak - kind of. and I can stay awake for more than 5 minutes at a time! Hurray! We still cough a bit but we are working on it. Now it is time for a long and blisteringly hot shower!!! Ciao, babies!!!

10/26/2005
Coughing, well it is that or being unable to breath so - its coughing or dead. I am seriously thinking of making coughing a hobby - we seem ot be doing so much of it. But really - we ARE getting better! Oh dear! Too much Monty Python! No we aren't going for a walk. Get that cart out of here! And put me down! Stop it!

Anyone need an office dweeb? My son, long may he wave, out of Penn State, needs employment so he gets out of my house! He's 6'6", approx 220, likes wearing suits (go figure) and ties, reasonably cute and ,amazingly enough, a diligent and intelligent worker. Previously worked at that 5 sided building - you know the one. If you cannot offer him a job - at least get me a case of that spray "Kid-B-Gone".

I have been found out! Halloween candy is SUPPOSED to be for the munchkins who beleaguer your house on Oct 31st. It is NOT for the Nip to periodically snitch pieces from when no one's looking. Well, yes, they looked. BUT ITS CHOCOLATE! OK, ok, I will go out tomorrow and get some more. ALRIGHT! Jeez! You'd think I'd killed millions rather than just ate a few, ok ok more than a few, pieces of chocolate.

You will recall that we had a little brake trouble with Cat's Yukon a while back? As in no brakes? Well it has been in the shop for all of this time (A month? For brakes?) and it appears that we are still awaiting parts - parts that work. Ever see a man separated from his truck before? And my Expedition goes into the shop for that noise in the back end this Friday but I have a spare F150 so my case is not as dire as his. My poor darling! - Ciao Babies, Love you, Let's do lunch?

10/26/2005
Update. My Expedition threw its gears this afternoon. There I am creeping towards Battlefield Manassas with agonizingly incremental slowness with fast headbanging music slamming from the speakers. The irony was not lost. Anyone have spare funds to the tune of a third world country's annual budget so I can get this beast back onto its tires? Oh, what the hell, skip the mortgage! You will not have to worry about me running you off the road now. The MGB is way kewl and tougher than my case-hardened heart but it does only have 4 cyls. Ah well. I am sure I can get all the groceries into it even if I have to balance a bag or two in my lap. The gods must truly love me! KISSES!!

10/27/2005
Today I met the wonderful and gorgeous G!!! And she's such a NICE lady too!! I hope your day wasn't too awful G. My fingers are crossed for you hun!

Stage 3, the final one, has been achieved!! My hair is fabulous! Thank you, G for the secret!! Worth every minute and every penny!

Unfortunately the Expedition will be VERY expensive so, shrugs, I will do what I can but you may not see me very often for awhile. Cat's truck is finally, ready (just in time?) so we have to get that one out first. Not as expensive as mine but not cheap either. More later!

10/28/2005
Heard back on my truck. It has been stuck in 4x4 low. No telling why or how much damage has been done but they're looking at it. Going to get Cat's from the shop later today. Then its groceries and paying the phone bills. TGIF hell if it is! that's bill paying day!

Tomorrow's the party and I fully intend to enjoy myself esp since Cat's driving. Not sure about what his costume will be. Perhaps dress all in black with a mask and say he's a 'cat burglar'?

Anyone remember the Feeling Like I'm Fixing to Die Rag? Just renewed my acquaintance with it. Hilarious and rather sad. Much like most of the blogs in here. We are supposed to be having fun here, people!!! Very well! Since you all have decided to be stubborn! The whippings will commence and continue until all of your morals have improved! Line forms on the left. No pushing. Wait your turn quietly. There's a good person! WHACK, WHACK, WHACK! ...Next!

10/29/2005
I drive a 1998 Ford Expedition. Usually. But this week it threw its gears - so I thought and I ran it to the dealership. Well the gears may or may not be okay but the 4x4 motor, the rear transfer case and

the rear end itself all need to be replaced. The final bill will be in the region of $5k. All without any guarantee that the transmission will be okay. A tranny for this thing will run $3600 installed. SIGH. I guess my pink leather domme' suit will just have to wait. But real life does have a way of interfering with a great sex life! I am now driving the 1974 1/2 MGB. This mean allowing extra traveling time as I do not care to take it much over 70mph. And should you call my cell when I am driving it, well, I will not be able to hear you so just use TM instead of voice. What do 'they' say? If it has tires or testicles, you're going to have trouble with it? Well one thing, those with testicles are a lot cheaper to look after!

10/30/2005
Halloween party? Oh, yes! That party where I didn't win the raffle, ah well, kissed 4 men, danced with 3 men and interviewed 2 men much to Cat's amusement, and was invited - once I had ditched Cat - to a hotel room. Hah! Like THAT's ever going to happen! Lose one of the few men who can and will catch me hurtling into his arms? I don't think so!

Remind to call Frank again tomorrow morning around 11am please.

Taj party this Friday!!! Now you will get to see my costume!! Wheeeeeeeeee! Hope you like it!! Ciao, my darlings!!!

10/31/2005
HAPPY HALLOWEEN !!!!!!!!!!!!!!!

NOVEMBER
2005

11/01/2005

Decisions, decisions - there are two parties to choose from this Friday 1. the Taj with friends, or 2. a house party with people we don't know. You can see the dilemma. This might be one of those 'coin flip' moments! If Taj then I get to see my friends, perhaps play with them and might even win the costume contest. If houseparty, play is guaranteed but no friends and no costume contest.

Remind me to call Frank this Thursday, please

Group rules to live by: women - give each man there his sexual opportunity; men - offer something sexual to every woman there. Oh, and personally, I would have waited until the evening was over to hunt for my hood ring if I had one. Delay sex for jewelry? I don't think so! But should you find an earring anywhere, you might want to ask me first. Note to self: leave the emeralds in the vault. Wear the cheap stuff. OK got it.

11/02/2005

This all began because I hate flip-phones. The Nokia 6682 was advertised by a particular cellular phone company and I signed up for two (cost $600). Waited. Waited. Called - on back order. Waited some more. Called again -cancelled. The phones are too old. What? They just came out October 15th! They still support the phones for those who have them and should I go and get them on my own they would support me as well. But it seems that Cingular and Nokia have had a falling out. Okay, so I asked after the Motorola ROKR as seen on tv. Sorry but we do not have in inventory. Okay! Went elsewhere and bought two Nokia 6682 (cost $719),

Cingular returning my $600 and I keep my old plan (same same same) which cannot be bettered. All because I wanted a phone I didn't need a microscope to read and one that doesn't fold in half and get lost in my playbag.

Remind me to call Frank tomorrow please.

After discussion, we have decided to go to the private house party this Friday. You will not see my costume. Ah well! It was very fetching. Two couples decided to join in with us so John's expecting 6 more people instead of the one he had bargained for. Oh, the dear man asked if I would like him to set aside a room for me in case I wanted to enslave men. Wasn't that nice of him? Such a sweety!

PS the delay due to jewelry was not, I repeat, not about the jewelry - it was about delaying sex! Honey - it is all I can do to wait until they get their clothes off!!!!!! Ciao, babies!!!

11/03/2005
Well, I thought the cell phone issue was resolved. HAH! Bought the phones, received the order confirmation email at 22hrs; then at 23:54 hrs received an email saying order was cancelled. HUH? Called them back. They had thought I wasn't me. I proved that I was indeed me and the order is once again on. I have an order confirmation email again. Went to UPS and there it was in Dallas Tx. The phones are due here tomorrow. I will check again in a few minutes.

I will call Frank circa 11am today - cross your fingers for me!!

Cat's truck is back and all fixed! Very nice! Mine is still in the shop where it most likely remain for awhile. SIGH! The MGB is way kewl however so I will not repine. Instead I will set about trying to gather up $5k. How are my stocks doing? Hmmmm. Ciao, darlings!!

11/07/2005
The new cell phones have arrived and I am currently wrestling with them since they do so much more than my old ones - have to figure out how it all works! New technology can be fun if I can just get the right sequence of buttons pushed!

Remind me to call Frank this Wednesday.

New pix from last Friday's house party have been posted! Wow, did we have a GREAT time!! Sorry we had to miss the Taj but when some cuties call - well, you know how it is with us - we cannot resist!! Get naked!! Thank you so much for inviting us and keep us on your guest list for next time!!! Where I shall, once again , wave my tail *w*!

Ciao, babies!!!

11/08/2005
The foreplay begins when the date is set. I spend some time wondering this and that. I revisit their profile and gawk at the pix. I email and chitter chat. Then there's the prepping before the date and the drive over with both of us speculating how it will be. So by the time we hit their front door, I am on a

106

slow long simmering heat setting. The twin V-12s are idling! So foreplay? Just take your clothes off, baby!

Call Frank. Call Frank. Call Frank.

At least tonight I get to spend a quiet evening within the loving circle of his arms! My darling Cat will keep me all snuggly warm and cozy! We all should be independently wealthy so we could all live like this ALL of the time! He even doesn't mind it when I snore! LOL

11/09/2005
Excellent news, G! Glad to hear that all went well! You will find that you love your new found freedom.

Yes, yes, I will call Frank! Thank you! I also have to call L. Yes, and meet this person for lunch. What else? Hmmm. Buy new undies and lounging jammies. Get the stilettos fixed.

The truck, remember my expedition?, is still in the shop awaiting parts. OKAY. I see how this will be. Thank goodness because I have to scrape up some more money to pay for the repairs. Almost there! Buy more oil for the MGB for whom one tank of gas also means one and one half quarts of oil - you know what that means.

Tomorrow will be a busy afternoon and evening *w*. Well, my tight schedule usually becomes even more constricted during this time of year - you may have noticed that I am not at the Taj as often as usual. Weekday evenings work best for us during the winter. So off I go!

11/10/2005
Dylan had it right - do not go gentle into that good night. Each of us has within him/her the urge to dance naked in thunderstorms - so go right ahead! Often it is this sort of thing that is the most attractive about a person. That odd kick in your gallop! The grin - you know the one - that says "I am a bad boy/girl" Leap into his fervid arms! Go on! He won't mind! Gather her up in your arms and do a slow dance in the kitchen! Meet his eyes across the room and silently share the joke. Often times the small things are the sweetest.

Called Frank. Had to leave a message. Was bad - didn't call L.

So much to do that I had better get busy and do it esp since I will be busy this afternoon and evening. Busy, busy, busy. Kisses all around! Ciao, babies!

11/11/2005
^5 to my fellow veterans !!!

11/14/2005
I suppose that I must not be terribly social. When we go to these clubs etc. most people seem to need hours of chatter and then begin to play around midnight. Now, this would not be a problem except that I have to leave by midnight. Bearing these time constraints in my mind, I am ready to play as soon as I get in the door, get a drink and get my clothes off. Anyone else have the same problem? Perhaps we should get together? Anyone else a 'self-starter'?

call Frank call Frank call Frank

Ah! but it is time for dinner! Daughter called from Bama - doing well - so that's good. Son remains unemployed beyond seeking employment - we all need clients - life continues in other words! More later!

11/16/2005

Just so you'll know - we are NOT heading to Tabu this weekend. Friday night at the Taj instead. You know us - we are the ones who were belting out David Lee Roth's Just a Gigolo one night last summer and me a heavy metal lover! Cat's more eclectic.

Frank's going to call me back today. Maybe. It could happen.

Met the most wonderful couple last evening! And THEY were the ones who told US that we were wearing far too many clothes! Finally a couple even faster self-starters than we are! WHEEEEEEEEEE! Had a great time! Looking forward to seeing them again! Ciao, babies!!!

11/17/2005

"Love to eat those Bambis; Bambis what I love to eat. Bite they little heads off; nibble on they tiny feet." Thank you Killban. Being without a lot of moisture, venison tends to become dry when its cooked, so stewing it or wet roasting it are the best cooking methods. Now if it were bear, you would have to use not only the dry roasting technique but would have to elevate the meat on a rack thus allowing the fat to fall away from the meat. Bear meat tending to be fatty. Of the two, bear is much richer and gives you more bang than the buck.

Frank is supposed to call me sometime today.

The Expedition comes out of the shop today! Hurray, hurray, hurray! I must call and alert them! Make sure the spark plugs were changed and the state inspection done as well as the repairs. Thank heavens the tranny is okay! It was just the 4 wheel drive system that needed to be fixed. soon I will be warm and listening to music while I drive!! YES!! Watch out, fellow drivers!!!

11/18/2005
I love my truck. I love my truck. I love my truck. I love my truck. I love my truck. I love my truck. I love my truck. I love my truck. Not that I would go so far as to kiss it on its hood. I love my truck. I love my truck. I love my truck. I love my truck. I love my truck. I love my truck.

Frank says to call him Tuesday. He also said Bill's getting twitty. Please don't get twitty, Bill darling! You know I love you. Not as much as my truck of course. But hey!

Today's schedule includes, having lunch with a man, moving money, getting groceries so Cat doesn't stand in front of the pantry lamenting the lack of food therein (but there are raisins and Diet Cokes!), and perhaps the Taj tonight but that's after I run Cat through his exercises *w*. Ciao, babies!!!

11/21/2005

110

Did the Titan Arum Lily at the Botanical Gardens - very special and yes it reeked but I am tough. Fascinating plant though! Huge flower too! I have never been frisked going into a botanical garden before either. Tis a new world, my pretties!

Call Frank Tuesday. *crossed fingers here* And thank you for the laughs 82nd! And your pix *eg - which were 'enlivening' to say the least!

More parties upcoming! Love it! House and hotel parties preferred to the club scene. Anyone know of a hotel with contiguous suites? Connecting suites I suppose they would be called? All info, and invites, cheerfully accepted!

11/22/2005
Yes we would be interested esp if not also on Friday evenings. This is such a busy time of year. Party this Saturday! Then a lazy afternoon with some new friends on Sunday. Huge fuck fest on the 8th (dare I mention that bona fide single guys are welcome?) and another party on the 10th and I am not quite sure it the next one's the 11th or the 14th but it is to be vanilla and I will find out.

Call Frank Call Frank Call Frank oh! and also call the lawyer

Now then tis a question of liability I am sure but the garage disconnected my cruise control on my truck, to prevent its bursting into flames, but the parts are not due in until February!!! So they will have to compensate me for the lack of utility of my SUV, the increased gas usage, devaluing my vehicle and whatever else I can come up with. Will write Ford a letter! It might work.

11/22/2005
Sorry guys but these orgies have been keeping me busy of late. I have not had time to take notes. Let us just say that various men have been enjoyed in various ways - I will leave the rest up to your, no doubt, fertile imaginations. No you may not lick the back of my knees - you evil teddy bear, you! Hey, I am trying to blog here! Back, back! *fending him off* And stop leaking testosterone! Tis most unfair! (Note: never try to blog when a slut is lingering about esp if he's naked.) And no, stroking you cock whilst saying 'here kitty, kitty' is not going to work! Well. Perhaps it will work. hmmmm ....

11/23/2005
We prefer meeting other couples almost anywhere BUT at a club or M&G. A houseparty or one on one seems much more the thing to us. Not that M&Gs are not fun but they do tend to be impersonal.

Yes, the 'Here Kitty, Kitty' worked! Okay? Happy now? As if I ever could resist Cat!

I agree w you S, darling! KISSES!

I am currently juggling money and arrangements for my next orgy., reference to which seems to have escaped notice - oh well! I will just have to make do with the men who signed up *eg*. Thank you, fellas! Ciao babies!!!

11/24/2005
HAPPY THANKSGIVING !!!!!!!!!!!!!!!!!!!!!!!!

11/25/2005

What book? Why wasn't I told about this? If I had known I would have made sure I was lovelier and more witty! Jeez! These people just don't give you time to prepare! Did my pictures turn out alright? Where's my signed advanced copy? Damn, I miss all of the good stuff! I should call my agent! To all of you budding diarists, journalists, and authors out there - make sure you give me at least a chapter in which you only say the nicest things about me!

Frank says to just be patient and wait my turn. *sighing deeply*

Pursuant to one of my blogs herein, guys do not stand shoulder to shoulder naked and stroking saying "Here kitty, kitty!" at the next houseparty! Cat's been laughing himself sick over the idea and I am having the gravest misgivings! That's the last time I will tell you all anything! Besides which, I just might take you all up on the offer and THEN where would you be?

11/28/2005

More rain; just when the temperature moderates too. Went shopping for a long-sleeved sheath dress - the ladies know what I mean - and all I found were sexy black lace and other be-frilled, numbers more suitable for a New Year's bash amidst lifestylers. Well, Cat's eyes lit up at the thought of seeing me wearing them. No miniskirts after age 35? HAH! I wonder if they have my size? And I am not going to tell you where or what store so you cannot snap it up before me! Let us all hope that the c. card has enough room on it!

Tis the final quarter of the year - so get yourselves to your advisors, cpas, etc etc etc. and get your affairs in order for the coming onslaught by the IRS. If you do not have advisors, cpas, etc. - go out and get yourself some. I know of a few who would not blink an eye at your lifestyle - and a few who are in it.

The hotel party proposed for this past weekend was a bust. Unfortunately I had to call them to find this out. Last minute changes send me to my list and I personally call each person to give them the latest but perhaps this is just a manifestation of my 'control issues'. I do hope the lady who wasn't feeling well soon gets better. More parties!!! Ciao, babies!

11/29/2005
Well, the c. card obliged so now I am the proud owner of a lovely, be filled, be-sequined, slinky little black dress - really what other color is there for me? I have to be very careful wearing it because if Cat's reaction is any indicator, I will not be wearing it for long. Another, more domme, outfit I purchased had to be returned - too short lengthwise in the torso. There is some length to me. I wonder if anyone will take me seriously in pink leather? I shall have to ask Tina about it. I am going to have to return to the more traditional dress and pearls for this one vanilla dinner party - we have a heavily social weekend planned, Dec 8 - hotel party, Dec 9th at the Taj, Dec 10 party at the Taj and then 11th the dinner party vanilla style.

I am thinking of changing my section of 'describe yourself' to "ancient, gnarled and gravely debilitated" what do you think?

Had a debate recently with another 40-ish woman who was convinced that my pictures could not possibly be mine. Perhaps more of an argument than a debate - a discussion, then. Yes, I do look like that as some of you lovely people can testify. I attribute it to good genetics, a good attitude, poor diet, smoking, drinking and having wild rampant sex with skilled and enthusiastic men as often as is possible! Speaking of which...Oh, Cat !!!

11/30/2005
Sorry but cowgirl boots have three strikes against them 1. too girly-girl, 2. too 'good girl', and 3. don't need 'em when I have my stiletto'd heeled black leather ankle boots both high heeled and kitten heeled. Yeah, I bite. And you love it! You know you do!

So this book is called <u>Swingers' Diary</u> then? Wonder if my local library can loan me a copy? And if all of the blogs bear some resemblance to reality the book may even be accurate! You may think I haven't been paying attention, but you would be incorrect.

Single males are very useful when fleshing out, can I use that term?, one's MMMMMMMMMMMF party roster so don't knock them! My latest party is going to be 7 women and circa 21 men. I hope that's enough? I don't want the ladies to feel slighted by too few eager men. That would never do! And here you thought we were just fluffy-bunnies! - Ciao, babies!

DECEMBER
2005

12/01/2005

Nip/Tuck? Isn't watching the political scene enough gruesomeness for you? Witness Mr. Cunningham having his tuck nipped! Tsk tsk tsk. Which reminds me - do not nip men's tucks - they tend to squeak about it - I just get so into it you see that I *ahem* get 'carried away'. It is Atkins approved and I rarely do eat lunch so you see how it happens. I just wish men were more 'generous' as 10 cc.s isn't enough. "Darling! Where are you going? I only want to......come on, just once more! I promise!"

Hmmmm 30 people and only 3 beds...sounds like a GREAT PARTY to me!!! Hope the guys amp up because the ladies sound like they're maxing revs even now!

Oooops! Cat reminds me that I have knitted my schedule. It is this Friday, not next, that is my Taj night. Every other Friday during the winter months. On my off Fridays I cut Cat loose so I can get some things done here while he goes forth and keeps us in the public eye. Much like when my other partner in crime and I split up so we can do two bang parties instead of just the one. Did I just say too much?

12/02/2005

Hmmmm one lady out, one possibly two in. And I still have a house to clean. Groceries - don't forget the groceries and that check to charity oh and we'll need to get to IKEA for a build a bed thing since we are one bed short this year. People are coming to us for the holidays this year - its our turn. Personally, I think the antique bed stored in pieces in the basement would do just fine but someone's worried about its effect upon his decor! Mail the cards and

118

gifts. Get some more gifts - yes, this year I didn't get my shopping done in August as per usual. Then its gather receipts for the tax lady, lose 30 lbs or so, find more clients, mail out pkgs to current clients and write up newsletter due out in Jan. And I still haven't cut back my peonies! In other words - a typical Friday for me! TGIF? I don't think so!

Giving my new dress a trial run tonight. Black, sexy, sequined, and frilled. - tell me what you think.

And it is time for me to review Estate Planning as I have a test next week. Once that's passed, it is time for the end of course exam. Once past that, its time to study for the big certification test next year. Oh, and pay my annual fees. Again. APG is a vacation for us!! That's why we like you all so much!!!

12/05/2005
We tried using the wishlist and sending those notes but we got zero response back to these tentative overtures so we stopped using it. It is a nice thought - sending someone a note saying, in essence, nice profile, you seem like someone with whom we could share common interests. But apparently people are offended by such non-committal notes. Fine. But as I read the blogs, they are also offended by notes expressing a strong and committed interest. Kindly maketh up thy mind.

Playing with words: polymathematical polyamorists. Describes us rather well.

The dress seemed to get a lot of positive response. Shame it is so very hard to wear and suffered from sequin leakage. The other outfit that I was going to return - the company has a 20% restocking fee and I have to pay return shipping. Not worth it so if any of you smaller ladies would like a rad leather outfit guaranteed to raise a man's pulse rate to dangerous levels - let me know.

12/06/2005
The reason people enter into these situations and then go and write books about it is that real life is magnificently more intricate and amazing than imagined life. Research has to be done. Bases must be covered. Memoirs of a salacious life are far more interesting to people than memoirs of a Stepford person. Shrug it off and move along - nothing to see here. Of course, I am just jealous because they didn't put me in their book. If I had time, I would pout.

Alliteration: fulsome felines following fluffy fat french finches filching fat-free french fries from Fred's fingers

Its not a red dress - in fact it is a black leather and black fishnet teddy - and yes it will raise his blood pressure if he sees you in it - just beware, if you are long waisted, it will not fit you vertically. I said RAD not RED. *ahem* excuse me, I didn't mean to yell. Must remember my daughter's mantra for me "Serenity. Serenity". Now that we have all calmed down, and I have explained about the bed purchase - we are okay. I am glad I didn't strangle him. Close, he came very close this time but no throttling yet. Perhaps next week! Ciao, babies!

120

12/07/2005

How's this for a kick in the head? Got a call yesterday afternoon. Daughter - the one in Bama working and going to school, you remember her I am sure - has gone and married him! Surprise, surprise. Apparently they got the license, waited however long they had to, then took a free lunch hour and got married by his grandfather the Baptist minister. We have nothing against the colt but we don't like the stable, ya know? Now I am someone's mother-in-law !!! Can you imagine? I think I feel old.

In order to separate your paragraphs insert a < and then a P and finish up with a >. I put this small set of symbols on its own line. Got it?

Party, party, party. Now we have two to attend in one evening. I have delegated the decision to Cat. - he's feeling old too, btw - we will see what his decision is later today. Still waiting on the proctor to take my test - has to be passed by Dec 26th. What else is up in the air? Contracts not yet implemented but I did manage to squeak a small profit out this year - my own biz you know, which is not bad for a brand new small company's first year. No bank financing of course. Also no salary but hey I have some available income that covers bills and food. Sasha the dog's not well - allergic reaction to something, vet's dealing with it but slow recovery. Lets see, what else remains open? A few more gifts required. Time to mail stuff out. SO - onward and upward! Ciao, babies!!

12/08/2005

I could not agree with you more. It is not until they are 40 years old that a man realizes the value of not having groundless self-satisfaction and the value of paying attention to who she is not just to what she is. But then, I have always been inordinately fond of the 40 year old teddybears; those warm, confident, furry men that a lady can joyfully take to bed with her.

More movie controversy - this time about Narnia, last time about Harry Potter - didn't anyone notice the same old pagan virtues in both? From the Stoics you know - witness the Meditations of Mark Anthony.

Party, party, party time! Unfortunately there are rules about this sort of thing - when conflicting parties arise, you go with the first that invited you. Thank you, Miss Manners and Aunt Agatha. Look darlings it is far too cold for me to dress sexy - you are getting matching sweater and slacks with the black leather kitten heeled boots. We wouldn't want me catching cold now would we? Still feeling old but I hope that today's orgy dispels that. *EG* 6 women, 16 men, and only 3 beds. YEEEHAW!!!

12/09/2005

Its morning, its cold, and it is the 'morning after' - but WOW what a great party it was!!! Sorry but my personal best record remains unbroken - not that I didn't try - but we had two who RSVP'd yes and then didn't show. 5 women, 12 men and 3 beds. A good time was had by everyone; a later arriving Cat grinningly said he could hear me from halfway down the hall! Thank you all for cumming! If you hear a woman laughing as you read this blog entry - its me.

So today's agenda is a trip out in the snow wastes of VA for groceries - an expedition in my Expedition!

This is the two party weekend so I am definitely taking today off. Someone has to clean up around here! We have like-minded persons tomorrow and the vanilla persons (those OTHER people) on Sunday. Tree decorating tonight! The turkey I bought is too big so will have leftovers. The house has been decorated already. - Just running down my checklist here. - buy some more gifts, mail out those ready to be sent - you know the sort of thing. Celebrate!!

12/12/2005

Okay I have looked over this week's schedule and its going to be BUSY! Calloo Callay! Fun with friends old and new. But first, the dinner party report! Oh my! How very staid we were! 6 persons chattering away on topics various being polite while the beef got overdone. Imagine being intimidated by a piece of beef. Hmmm, just open The Joy of Cooking I'd say. Heat oven to 400, place beef on rack in pan fat side up, place into oven and immediately turn heat to 350 degrees then it is 18 minutes per pound for medium rare. Easy peasy. So we had pre-prepared standing rib roast with bottled gravy, already prepped carrots lightly candied, and green beans with sliced almonds and generic red wine. I am guessing they don't cook much. Tried drawing out my hostess but was only partially successful as we have very little in common. Ah well, perhaps one day.

Inconsistent profiles are a bane. Please review and see if you've said one thing and done another. Its no good saying you are up for everything or anything if your verbiage says something else or all of your pix are locked.

Note: hopefully the high drama experienced at Saturday's party will be avoided but a timely warning is in order for those who are diabetic. Please be very careful when drinking alcohol. If you don't get your system balanced just so - someone will be calling 911 as happened last Saturday night. Luckily, she made it. A timely call saved her. Thank you, JK - you're a good man! Ciao, babies!

12/13/2005
Its only Tuesday and already the schedule has changed. Last night's couple flaked on us and tonight's male has a cold so that's no good. He delayed until it became evident that he wasn't getting over it to call and cancel but at least he called. This means another workout for Cat. Mmmmmm pounce!

Since last Thursday's party was a hit - we will be having another in late January.

Our parties are all about sex, of course. Women with huge appetites are already asking to come and indulge. Yes, really. Offer her a 3 to1 or 5 to 1 ratio and see her eyes light up. Ditch the husband at the door and select from the buffet, ladies! Yeah, there's pressure. EG You can socialize during the intermissions. Every man offers something sexual to every woman. Every woman gives every man his chance. If she has to go out and drag them back to the bed - so be it! We were thinking of having nametags for the men only they'd most likely have to stick them to their rumps "Hi! My name is Mark" Perhaps printed programs? The best comment from the last party is the one S told Cat - "Look, if you want a decent blowjob, you're going to have to stop telling jokes!"

12/14/2005
Sorry I'm late but I had some things to get done. Well of course you can say whatever you please but equally true is that they can reply whatever they please and so it goes. If you're going to say it - then prepare for the heat from those others. No big thing - you don't have to sleep with them ya know.

Next sex party is Jan 26th.

Well Tues and Thurs got cancelled due to them having colds. *sigh* very bad timing - I really wanted to see them! I mean REALLY wanted to see them. Poor Cat will now just have to take the heat himself. There's no rest for him! Besides, cumming that often is supposed to be good for you, dear! I know they said three times a week, but certainly 9 times cannot hurt! And if nine times doesn't, why not try for 21 times? Don't go saying 'down girl to me!"

12/15/2005
I dislike exercising - other than sex, of course - so this morning's been a drag but 'the enemy' (aka the scale) says that I must so I must. A case of if not now - When? so I did it. Tunes to exercise by NIN's Closer, Papa Roach's Scars, and Morissette's Fear of

Bliss to begin with. Rob Zombie's Dragula and Living Dead Girl (Naked Exorcism Mix) next. Oh! Sorry was chatting with a man - when I met him, I hung back a bit - twas all of 5 minutes before I was removing his clothing. Ah! Nothing like discussing old times!

you can come to our sex party if you're cute and willing to play by our rules

Today it is back to get my hair touched up. Think kind thoughts as I battle my way through this week's storm. I hope those other people will not drive too horribly! It gets very frustrating - esp when you don't have the remotely controlled 50 cal mounted on the roof. Messy - but effective. Ah well! I shall have to make do. Then a spot of shopping and its curl up with Cat for a night of fun at home – purrrrr, purrrrr, purrrrr. Ciao, babies!

12/16/2005
Okay, okay am back after doing another 20 minutes aerobics - ugh! Dreadful. Thanks for the encourage-ment and it may come to pass as you say but I strongly have my doubts. If twere true, I would never have stopped doing it in the first place. Logically speaking.

Am going to beat senseless anyone who wants me to shave down there - currently revisiting why I don't Grrrrrrrrrrrrr

A day of nice weather and moderated temps! Great - but just a teaser for the next round of sub-zero days I fear. Enjoy it while it lasts. Xmas party at the Taj tonight! I am not dressing up as an elf!!! Then

126

you will not see me until the 30th of December. "The Invisible Nip!" Enjoy yourselves!!!

12/18/2005
Hmmm. such a debate! I go for Happy Holidays myself. Well look at it from this point of view; the solstice has always been worshipped, tis winter and if you made it this far and still had food stored - you were assured of surviving the winter. Cause for celebration - oh yeah! Thus began the Saturnalia which led to Christmas. On a parallel development we took over the Xmas tree from tree worshipping Germans. BTW Xmas the X is the sign of the cross there so it is religious too. Religious shorthand. I haven't made a detailed study of the other religious holidays yet and so refrain from speaking of them.

The separation of church and state is for the preservation of the church. Power corrupts. Watch the opening scenes of Elizabeth to see what happens when church and state are one. Picture US M1 Abrams tanks rolling over your house because you attended the wrong church. That's what separation of church and state means. It does not mean banning plays from schools. Churches must be without political power and the state may not endorse one religion over another. So crèche scenes belong on church grounds. Santa Claus belongs on state grounds - and long may they both endure!!

HAPPY HOLIDAYS

12/19/2005
Had a quiet weekend which was just as well since the holidays are upon us. Today it is gingerbread fish-shaped muffins (let no icon be neglected) and

mince meat pies. Final decoration of the tree has been accomplished. Almost all of the gifts bought - now for the stocking stuffers. The the wrap-fest and placing of packages beneath the tree is next. Begin thawing the turkey Friday. Husband shops Saturday. Final housecleaning etc also Friday and Saturday. Wheeeeeeeeeeeee!

next trip to Taj is the 30th

Our parties are also for couples who are seriously into separating at the door and the women have to be into both quality and quantity as we look for at least a two men to each woman ratio. Thank you to the single men who showed interest. We will let you know if the ladies have selected you. Three seriously capable women thus far. The 'open enrollment period' ends on the 20th of December. The volunteer list will be circulated amongst the women on the 2nd of Jan. Final selections will be due the 10th. Invitations with all details will be sent out on the 15th. RSVPs due back NLT Jan 20th. Party Jan 26th. Get ready to rumble!

12/20/2005
Bake a mince pie, clean up the house, prepare the beds for guests. Just checking my list. Unfortunately meeting people is not one of the items on it. That will have to wait until the 30th at the Taj. Just not enough time. Have to find stocking stuffers too. Buy a gift for the boy and several for the husband. Might just have to go to Sears and get him tools. Why is it that shiny metal means tools for guys but jewelry or bullion for women? And my truck is low on gasoline.

may strangle Cat -though it isn't indicative of goodwill towards men

I am doing something on Wednesday...oh yes! Testing! Perhaps I should review the material? Have to pass these little tests so I can go on to the big test. Add to the list - Review the Material. Last day for the open enrollment period. Paid the water bill yesterday. There are a million things to do and they have outlawed cloning!! Drat them!! I could use being in several places at once right about now. Ciao babies and Merry Christmas!

12/21/2005
Ah! The solstice! From this point forward the days will lengthen and the blessed heat will begin its return. The volunteering for the party period has now ended. Thank you to all of those who offered their services. The list will go out to the ladies on Jan 2nd. They will select those with whom they wish to play and the invitations will be sent on Jan 15th. I am organized because I have to be but, yes, my office remains a mess. Well, something has had to give!

You remember Frank? The man I was always calling? Pray for him; he is now battling a new menace - liver cancer.

You will all be happy to know that I have not strangled Cat. Being a very quick-witted, mildly evil teddybear, he managed to extricate himself - so he's now out of danger. Ever notice how hard it is to be angry with someone when he makes you laugh? MEN!! And they say they cannot dance! In my opinion, some of them dance far too well! And usually just out of reach! It is a shame they are so damn cute! Come back here! You cannot do that and then scamper away! Excuse me there's someone I have to do.................Cat!

12/22/2005
Well, the gingerbread muffins in the shape of fish did not turn out completely as we would have liked - they are fish but he cooked them too long. Just a trifle. More like thick gingerbread cookies now. Anyway - still tasty! Our huge Xmas gathering has once again dwindled. My daughter and hubby cannot come, son's gf cannot come and older brother (mine) cannot come - has to work. So it is just my Mommy who's coming - sometime today!! Quick clean the house and polish the furnace!!

The hotel party has been oversubscribed - too many people? Is that even possible? YES it is, so please stop!!!! there's Feb to consider.

The next Taj meet for me is 30th of Dec. Hope to see you all there. I have to finish up here and then go shopping etc. Busy, busy, busy. Just picture a tawny feline in a cardigan and gold rimmed half glasses (sliding down her nose) on one of those chains around the neck with a list and a pencil in her paws. For the modern age, also include the hands-free cell phone device behind her left ear and driving a large SUV at mach 3 with the stereo turned up to puree'. Can I still disappear at top speed leaving behind the cloud of hair pins? Ciao, babies!!

12/23/2005

130

Okay, I understand we are too old, too ugly, too fat, too cute, too intimidating, too slow, too silly, too kewl, too far away, too young, too short, he's too massive, not far enough away, she's too domme', too experienced, too fast, not cute enough, not experienced enough, we rotate cyclonically, and neither of us are bisexual –yeah, yeah, yeah -but we'd still like to meet you. If you should spin anti-cyclonically to our cyclonic rotation - well, PARTY!!

WARNING: EXCESSIVE SILLINESS FOLLOWS

EXUBERANCE - that you awaken every day is joyous; Celebrate it not just now but always - Run, my baby; run, my baby, run! - Dance, Sing, Play - LIVE LIKE YOU MEAN IT - so turn the carols up to puree' and sing along!! Crank the tunes and bebop while baking holiday treats. Beethoven's 9th at 80 million dbs is great for cleaning the house! Prevent your lover from exiting the bed with a flying tackle! Oh yeah! Find out who you are! There's no time to waste it. The light is GREEN, babycakes - go for it!! MERRY CHRISTMAS AND THE HAPPIEST NEW YEAR TO YOU ALL !!!!!!!!!!

12/27/2005
Excerpts from a recent conversation: "I didn't think I would feel comfortable in a group sex party. But I was! Being naked didn't seem to matter. It was like being at a dinner party but with a much tastier menu. I enjoyed it! I never thought debauchery could or would be so much fun! Now I find that I think all women are incredibly sexy, and attractive. Regardless of their size or shape, I find myself

enjoying everything about all women." I may have taken some literary license in writing the above but you get the gist of the thing. From walking around trapped in a tightly fitting box to a new freedom - this man has awakened! There is true joy in this life for those who can but see it.

12/28/2005
Sorry, just painted my claws so I wasn't listening to those disgruntled persons out there - you will have to bear with my unadulterated joi de vire (all spellings vague). Mon canard es en feu. HAPPY NEW YEAR!!!!!! and long may you wave that thing of yours about *eg* yes, THAT thing. 2005 was much as usual - up, down, and sideways; but now tis over and it is time to set in motion our evil plans for 2006. Did you write all of 2005 down in your diary hmmm? So your ancestors go OMG!!!! I did.

Awaiting the arrival of The Ethical Slut

Cat and I are sharing a cold right now so we must decline all play dates - we do not want to spread this stuff around, you know. Give us some time and we will be more than happy to make it up to you. How many times can a man cum in 45 minutes? Care to find out? Thus far we have 4 times at age 47. I am hoping to get more statistical evidence soon! I require one healthy male of each age to come and lie down right about here. That's it! Now I will just tie you down like so. Don't want you to run away and spoil my experiment. Are you comfortable? Good! Let us begin................

12/29/2005

I am very sorry to report that my condition has not improved. It is highly unlikely that I will be going anywhere for the next several days. This is not how I planned on doing New Years but one must needs when the devil drives. So I have taken my meds and will now return to my warm and cozy bed. Wake me at your peril.

12/30/2005
So this couple only replies to solicited emails? How do they solicited emails? Do they wear sandwich boards to parties? Do they ask random people in the street to email them? Perhaps they do it by sending unsolicited emails? OMG! And yeah, you are obligated to send something back - even if its a 'drop dead deluxe'. Think of it as someone giving you a compliment in person and you just giving them the cold shoulder. Treat others as you would like to be treated. In their case - we all may ignore their emails. "Oh look! an email from THEM. Ho-hum." delete.

Still not well - this will set my plans for world domination way back.

Son's girlfriend is coming to visit for the weekend - great timing! - and her parents are delivering her. Get to meet the whole crew then! This means that son is going to have to get the house ready since I am not well. It might be fun to watch - but you know I will end up helping out. But first - the grocery getting!!!

2006

JANUARY
2006

01/01/2006
"The damage caused by a few words spoken
Perhaps without thinking
Perhaps from a kind of fear
Continues as a poison and will not heal.

The overture made once and crushed
Is well remembered
Is accepted
Will not be made ever again.

The heart then closes around its core
The lesson well taught
The lesson well learned
Secrets kept far too secure.

We teach eachother over time
This far
This deep
Selecting pieces of persons.

The remainder wants out
To dance
To scream
This will not be permitted.

Remain then content
With what you get
With what you wanted
I will never ask. I will never tell."

01/03/2006
Now returning you to the regularly scheduled blog.
2005 was a good year overall but in 2006 we hope
to really blast off esp in our businesses. Thanks go
to Frank and, perhaps Bill. We shall see. I am really

138

hoping Richmond comes through as well. That would be a tremendous help to me. Patience is all that is required. Does Walgreen's sell Patience in capsule form?

To answer your questions - it never goes entirely away just becomes another layer. Think of your life as an encyclopedia upon the shelf - each volume having its own meaning and place in the series - that was an excerpt from vol.s 22 and 48 combined.

Son's girlfriend spent the weekend with us and she's DELIGHTFUL! We had a marvelous time. I do hope she picks up his option - she's perfect for him and fits into the family nicely! Well done, Boy!

I was going to put in a little something from page 112 from vol. 34 but have decided against doing so. Might skeer you all and we don't want to do that. Remember - naked Monopoly this Thursday - Ciao, babies!

01/04/2006
OK people you have GOT to read this book! The Ethical Slut by Dossie Easton & Catherine A. Liszt IBSN 0-890159-01-8. It is excellent! You will also enjoy it very much. Only you can prevent forest fires but with a little help from your friends you can both prevent them and toast your marshmallows too.

Frank made it! Hurray! Knew he was too ornery for liver cancer to win out! He was more forthright, of course; used the F word. We are having lunch next week in Georgetown. Anyone recommend a smoking restaurant?

Now then, are we all set for this Thursday's Naked Monopoly? You all are with me on this, right? Got your game sets, the other couple and all of the necessary sundries together? Good. Next month, we'll do Naked Twister if this 'game theory' stuff works out. Hey! Its either this or we'll have to have naked discussion groups on the Magna Carta or The Marshall Plan - your choice! Ciao, babies!

01/05/2006
Well, we have had to postpone the Naked Monopoly for a week. I also went and actually told some people what was written on page 112 of volume 34 - and they ran for the hills screaming "Noooooooooooo!! Stay away from me you horrible woman!!!!" I wish they would at least try it, you know what I mean? Limp penises? Yeah, and you cannot cope with that? Easy peasy. Just creatively use a vibe or have him do cunnilingus and call the dog simultaneously. You are only limited by your imagination. *EG*

not that I have any imagination, of course - well, any I can tell you all. You'd most likely run too. Tis why I write such clean blogs.

Fortunately Cat fears nothing and enjoys quite a lot of 'imaginative' things-Mmmmmmmmeow! So we are going to practice being 'imaginative' tonight - just in case another couple gives us an opportunity. Perhaps Cat will give me that 'guided tour' he's been promising me. I might even get my ankles licked again - you know I love that! Oh wait! This is supposed to be a clean blog! OK, OK getting mind out of the bed now. *wrench, shake* Ah! There we go! Book exchange at the Taj?

01/06/2006

Oh wow! Stay safe to those traveling. And hope all goes well to those undergoing medical treatment. Onto the topic of the day it seems - why penises refuse to play. Any number of reasons but a man's ability to thrill it NOT limited to his penis. I will admit that it is very, not to say extremely, easy to get me to cum - however the point remains valid. He still has his hands and his mouth and that devilishly clever gray mass between his ears. And if you really want to blow her mind, and her sensory capabilities, bring in a couple of your buddies and tackle her all at once. That will show her who's boss. *EG*

oh dear - seems I have slipped - you now know more than you need to - well, it will just be our secret. Shhhh.

Wild? No I am not wild. Un-inhibited perhaps but not wild. Oh no. Not me. Just ask Cat. Once he has recovered and regained the power of speech I am sure he will answer you. Honey?? You okay? Ah! That's good. You had me worried there for a minute. You may not be able to hear over the 'happy teddybear rumbles' of course. Such a happy man! Okay, okay I will clean it up. Clean blogs - only write clean blogs. You people have NO idea how difficult that is for me. Excuse me but, Cat's showing signs of life and he's just sooo cute! Mmmmmmmmeow!

01/09/2006

In looking over profiles I see a great many people putting limits on who they play with which is fine I suppose for those with a particular fetish but for us it has always been more of a questions of who you are. This is assuming that there is some degree of attraction between all of us. For me, Nip, if its large enough to get from you to me that's large enough. More important to me is if you know what to do with it once you get there. I am not a 'Size Queen'. I am perhaps a 'Performance Queen' but I dealt with that in the previous blog. Hey! This is the only exercise I really get! Well, it is the only exercise I ENJOY getting.

The February party will be couples only - more on this later.

The list for the January Party has been circulated to the participating ladies. Their choices are due back to me on the 10th and the invitations to those males selected will be sent out on the 15th. RSVPs from the men are due back by the 20th. Disease and death are the only excuses permitted for not showing once you have RSVP'd yes. Yes, I do follow Miss Manners' Guide to Excruciatingly Correct Behavior - how did you know? No shows are blacklisted. There are rules and they will be included in the invitation so I will not go into them here. Just wanted to keep all of those darlings who volunteered in the loop! Ciao, babies!

01/10/2006

Predators' existence is why we taught our children not to give up having a ferocious temper, they get it from their father, but to learn to use it more effectively. Being military brats, they understood the concept of effective power. My opinion is that any adult who sexually abuses or molests a child should get the death penalty, period. If not an adult and they sexually abuse or molest another child then we can go for incarceration for a period of time with counseling - depending upon circumstances. But the judge who gave that man 60 days for 4 years of repeated sexual abuse of a girl - he too should be shot along with the predator. I will not apologize for my attitude. While I have never been subject to sexual abuse, I have two children of my own. for whom I would cheerfully sacrifice the rest of the world's population to help.

Having been turned down again for not being bi - ladies, in light of the above - are you sure you would want me to be bi? *eg*

In light of recent news on the subject: a new biz opportunity - smoking only establishments! Only hiring smokers and only catering to smokers in nice comfortable, extremely well ventilated, and luxurious surroundings. Just think of the money you would pull in! This would eliminate having to stand outside in the fucking freezing cold more than 50 feet from the entrance so, heaven forefend, non-smokers should be subject to catching a whiff although they stand the same chance of dying from such as they do from a pot of geraniums falling from a third floor balcony. (stats from a British study). Now that I have been terribly controversial -

dontcha love it? - I will move on and go back to painting my claws. Ciao, babies!!

01/11/2006
Juggling dates and times trying to fit everyone in. I also have the party list results to tabulate. If Cat doesn't get this place cleaned up it will reflect badly on me. *eg* People will think less of me due to my poor housekeeping skills. The major issue is paper. There is simply too much of it. No, you cannot just shove it all into a box and hide it somewhere. Bonfires are out too. You will actually have to read the stuff and either toss it or file it. -that groaning you hear is Cat contemplating his immediate future. *says the woman who hired someone to do this for her*.

Broke a claw the other day. Unfortunately it wasn't on some man's back. *sigh*

Bill doesn't want to be my cat toy. He said so. He was such a nice man too - very disappointing. I had thought such a large tough guy could handle the tender mercies one small kitten like me. * looking harmless* Just a small bit of fluff, really. Surely, there's at least one big strong male out there who could endure? Winsomely yours, Nip

01/12/2006
Get in Touch With Your Inner Cat - walk around like the world's yours and lounge a lot looking very decorative. Occasionally, be and do something cute. Every now and again instill fear in the hearts of lesser beasts and kill something just because.

The next book on the list is The Moving Toyshop by Edmund Crispin. Highly recommended as being both very literate and yet hilarious with enough 'sight' gags and sly jokes in it to appeal to everyone! Please note the foot chase and the car chase. OH! and pay particular attention to Mr. Hoskins.

NAKED MONOPOLY TONIGHT - do not forget!!!! Not quite fit yet but as long as you don't kiss me- you'll be okay. The medicos tell me that I will survive. Very irritating however as I cannot feed off of the males yet to my satisfaction. I'll let you how much I won by tomorrow btw. *EG* You all do not stand a chance!! Ciao, babies!!

01/13/2006
NAKED MONOPOLY PRELIMINARY RESULTS - Cat came out the big winner, and this in spite of being heavily 'distracted' by two naked women in an abbreviated game, with $6,995.00 net worth. No one ended up with a monopoly although Cat did try to buy the remaining railroad not under his control from Bill who manfully resisted the allure of the vast sums Cat was offering. These robber barons! Tsk Tsk. Congratulations, darling!! Anyone else have results to report?

My usual driving pet peeves - I have added another to wit: Exit THEN Brake - or what did you think those long exit ramps are for?

MISC. Found a way to get men to vacuum - let them use the shop vac to do the job. Taking a lot of work to come to orgasm is NOT a virtue. Excuse me, I have to turn on the fish. Rolling orgasms are WONDERFUL! Curing colds via drinking scotch while sitting in the hot tub is fun! Good luck to all undergoing surgery. I did tell you to be careful when having sex on a trapeze. Ciao, babies!!

01/17/2006

I understand completely, dear! Been there, done that more times than I want to recall. Dual career military for 20 years. Those of us who do 'get it' are your support group, hun and yes, some days (nights) are worse than others. Feel free to mail anytime. Kudos to those who also 'stood up' and offered help. Interpersonal relationships - it is why we are here. HUGS!

Remind me to call Frank next Tuesday at 9 am - we are to do lunch that day. Thanks!

Well, its been the first year of my business and, lo and behold, I made a profit! Ah! Mind you, it was by the skin of my teeth but it is a profit. So now to begin year two. There's a very good chance for my business to take off this year. So wish me well! If it happens, I will throw one hell of a party! See you all at the Taj this Friday! Ciao, babies!

01/18/2006

Yet, funnily enough, Ayn Rand's hubby was not getting enough so I guess she thought sex was far too important to share with him. The anti-dictator tended to be dictatorial at home. Speaking of which, I recently heard that some people are offended by my being a domme'. If true, it is amazing. Wonder why they would care? They aren't directly affected. Cat just teases me about my "control issues" and thinks I am cute. *sigh* So hard to be taken seriously when wearing a matched set of pink lace underwear. Then the guys line up shoulder to shoulder facing me, stroking saying "Here, kitty, kitty!" while grinning. *sigh*

Three couples interested in February's party thus far. Almost have a quorum.

Having a spot of trouble in my garden- after 7 years the rhododendrons finally gave up. Lovely plants but it just was too wet for them last year. It might have been the lightning strike - I told you about that - that helped them out - but it means finding another species of large flowering shrub for shade. I will be planting an oak-leaf hydrangea down by the Japanese cherry tree this spring since its wet down there. It is time to lift and clean the iris but I will not be giving away any this year. I will be collecting empty coffee cans as they work best when bringing along baby iris - the metal ones. It is also time to collect the Rugosa offshoots to bring them along to replace the Hybrid Teas which do not like me. Picky, picky. I have decided to go with Adirondack chairs in yellow to match the deck this year instead of IKEA $10 sling chairs which simply do not last. I will still use the few sling chairs left as supplementary seating for polo though. And here you thought all I was interested in was sex. Ciao babies!

01/18/2006
We are NOT liars - we just gave ourselves permission to enjoy sex to the max and so we do!! Just put the head of your penis up against my g-spot and see how fast I cum!!! Wow!! Foreplay - takes too long - besides I have been dreaming about being with you ever since the date was made! So lets get

147

on with this!! Relax, breathe, give yourself over to pleasure !!!

01/19/2006
Group Sex Primer - While not for everyone, group sex can be marvelous fun for those willing to be adventurous. There are several styles of play parties from gb's to puppy piles. The basic methods you all know by now. (I hope so.) The thing is to do what feels good if its welcomed by the other(s) immediately involved. I suggest introducing yourself around and helping setting everyone at ease as you undress.

No one is keeping score here so take your time, slow down, relax and enjoy the spectacle if not actually playing at this moment. Take mental notes on what she appears to enjoy. See what seems to turn him on. When its your turn, you will have some idea of what to do.

If you move into a person's personal space and they hedge off or turn away - well, graciously try someone else. If someone propositions you feel free to say yes or no as you like. Just be friendly about it. No harm in asking. Do not just butt in or grab someone - use some tact.

If a couple, decide beforehand whether you are cruising together or separately. Remember to focus outward from yourselves if playing as a couple looking for a third or fourth partner. If your partner wants to just observe while you want to play, use the non-playing person as your 'wingman'.

148

If you would dearly love to but cannot, for whatever reason, focus upon outercourse as in caressing, kissing, cuddling, calling the dog, cunnilingus or fellatio - you know; everything but penetration. Perhaps later on or at the next party you can make good the 'rain check'. We aren't machines and we do understand.

If you bring toys, expect to share them or hold onto them with a death grip. Toys are very attractive and will get a lot of attention. Everyone has a play bag of some kind - I suggest leaving them in yours. This is also a good place to store your clothing and other accessories. Do not mess with another's play bag.

Safe sex is always practiced so get used to wearing your protection. We know its a bother but it beats picking something up and passing it along.

Your host/hostess will have made every effort to invite compatible people. All they ask is that you be a wonderful guest and have a good time.

01/19/2006
PETA never was known for having any real brains. For example, in addition to the deer example you cited, they released dairy cattle from their farm. Now, cows aren't very bright but modern dairy cows are completely unable to exist 'in the wild' - they require too much care and twice daily milking. The release resulted in the cows' deaths, not their 'freedom'. Minks released surprised PETA people by attacking eachother - they are carnivores you know and carnivores tend to be territorial. PETA itself also euthanizes 3/4 of the 'freed' dogs and cats. In almost ALL cases, animals "freed' by PETA end

up DEAD. IMO PETA exists solely to indulge the whims and feelings of people who do not like themselves or humans and know nothing about nature. PETA is NOT truly concerned with the care of animals.

Call Frank Tuesday at 9am. Call Frank Tuesday at 9am

The boy celebrates his 24th birthday today. He is also in danger of being employed. HURRAY! So he will soon be out of the house and into his own apartment. This will free up play space here. Ah! The freedom once the kids move out! I am savoring it now! Then we can stop 'sending him to the movies' when we wish to engage in adult fun and games. "Don't you have any friends?" "Here, take the car and go somewhere." "Just make sure to fill the gas tank before you bring it back." "Stay out for a couple of hours, okay?" Then I grab the scented body oil I developed for Cat and quickly run upstairs! Ciao, babies!

01/19/2006
What do you mean IF we THINK condoms work???? Of course, they work if properly fitted and properly used. You think Zip-Lock just came up with the idea for their baggies out of thin air? Plastic wrap that bad boy, baby!

01/20/2006
Ok - breastfeeding well, yes but - just let it go. A mutually beneficial arrangement although some of those benefits need not be specified. In fact, a lot of the benefits of mutually beneficial arrangements need not be specified. We won't go into them here

because I am shy. Hmmmm next thing you know, I will be wearing pink. Perhaps I'll also wear ribbons and bows.

Snuggled up with Cat afterwards and said I'd like some more. "Silly kitten, that's what gangbangs are for," was his reply. LOL

Polo season is coming up. First there are some point-to-points and timber races, and then the Spring Gold Cup races. Then there's the beach to consider - I have got to get my sunning in. It is time to put down the Pre-emergent on the lawns and check out the shrubs to replace the rhododendrons and the two dwarf Alberta spruces that also bit the dust. Once these #^$&& contracts are implemented I can DO something but not before. So very frustrating! But there's a party coming up next week *eg* so I'll get rid of the stress then! Gentlemen, prepare to defend yourselves !!!

01/23/2006
Not being shy, mousy, or small, come to think of it, men do not get grabby, ala N's problem, with me. No one smears cake icing on my breasts either. Lighten up I hear you say? It is all just fun? Yes, well we all have our own definitions of fun. But then someone crosses an invisible line and there we are another angry blog. The best advice fellows is to follow her lead and no further.

Call Frank tomorrow at 9am. Call Frank tomorrow at 9am.

I am so ashamed! I grow more scatterbrained by the moment! Any minute now and they will put me in a home! I hope the nurses are all very cute male teddybears in their 40s. *W* But Cat was highly amused so although I will never live it down it isn't all bad. What was bad was him dragging himself home at 7am. Tsk, tsk - talk about breaking curfew! Well, he was punished for that already so I will let it go. The party is 5 women and 13 men on 3 beds. Yeah we are fun but its in private people. And yes there will be cake. We still need three other cute and fun couples for Feb's party. Contact me soonest please!

I'd like to thank the single males who continue to write and ask that they hold off until the next open enrollment period whereupon we will again be asking for volunteers for March's party. February's party will be a couples only function. We are currently accepting couples who are seriously interested in heterosexual play on a more or less grand scale. Cake will be served since there's a birthday involved - yes, another birthday! All we ask is that you be ready, willing, and more than able. This includes the women too! No hanging back ladies! We have three couples now and are seeking three more couples. 6 men and 6 women and only 3 beds. Sounds like a party to me!

01/24/2006
This should be interesting. Although I usually play nice, you all are aware that I am one of THOSE women even if not one of the whip-swinging sisters. A lovely lady finds that she really would rather not, with her husband you understand, so she has called in a specialist - me. You see before you - fantasy fulfillment. The preliminary telephone interview went very well so we are meeting at their house

tonight to further discuss the parameters of the relationship. I understand I am also being consulted to improve his presentation skills so he will be able to offer himself up more effectively in the future. Easy peasy. This should be fun.

Called Frank at 9am he said call back in an hour - ok. We are to do lunch today.

And now a pet peeve. "I like men but I am only interested in doing my man. I am picky." Honey, that's not being picky, that's being pathetic. Licking the icing off the cake without eating the cake? Waste of our time. You go sit on the sideline and watch, then tell me how much fun that is. As opposed to what you could be doing? And no a blow job is not going to do it. Why are you even here? Sorry, but I hate it when people diss Cat like that. Think about it, the man must be amazing if he's kept my interest. Ciao, babies!!!

01/24/2006
One Very Happy Kitten! You may not know this, but I really, really, REALLY like men!!! The upcoming party where there will be 12 men to play with excites me immensely! I am like a kitten rolling in catnip! All of those lovely men willing to be sooo generous - ah! what fun!
Mmmmmmmmeow!!!

01/25/2006
Fantasy Fulfillment Interview Results - people, please do not skip over the basic skills and rush right on into fetishes. This just means some poor woman has to come along and begin from the beginning. Nice guy but poor to moderately compe-

tent in the basics. The things I do for friendship. Well, he will get his training but I am not taking him on as another of my men. When it comes to his adaptability training, I will need some ladies to pass him onto. These ladies need to be forthright about what they want and how they want it when. They can then pass him back. This will not be for some months though. *sigh*

Frank and I will be doing lunch this Friday

well time to go and get more groceries! Again! Yes, I know! Shocking how much time is spent getting groceries! They never last too! Tsk, Tsk. I suppose I do have to feed him however. Ah, well! No Taj this Friday as we have a b'day party to attend. Well off to the stores! Ciao, babies

01/25/2006
Yes, its a power thingy - just guy stuff. As for cliques, well, no one wanted us in theirs so we just made one of our own which anyone is welcome to join or not as the case maybe. We don't bite...........much. Newbies can always come up and say "Hello, I love you, Won't you tell me your name. " We smoke, we drink, and we will join in intercourse with as any people of the opposite sex as will fit onto the bed, floor, sofa, or from the chandelier (sp?). Any questions? If we don't know the answer, we will be happy to make one up just for you right there on the spot. The weekend's coming which is a good thing because Nip's slowly going insane due to a bureaucratic mix-up perpetrated upon her by the Commonwealth of Virginia long may she reign.

154

01/27/2006

Thank you to all of the generous men who entertained us so very, very well at yesterday's party! You guys were GREAT!! Sherry and I both had a MARVELOUS time!! WOW!!

Call Frank at 10:30

The Couples only party has been CHANGED from the 23rd to the 16th - got that? - the 16th beginning at noon venue to be announced once we have our quorum of 6 couples. We now have four couples all ready and willing to play. It's Nip's b'day you see. Champers will be served (not out of slippers) and we may even have cake too! We need two more 'adventurous' couples! No Taj tonight as there's a b'day party - yes, another one! but we will see you there next Friday. Ciao, babies!

01/30/2006

Nevermind; I have said that I will never again ask and never again tell. "The time has come," the Walrus said, "To talk of many things: Of shoes--and ships--and sealing-wax-- Of cabbages--and kings-- And why the sea is boiling hot-- And whether pigs have wings."

Today, today, today - call my daughter and Frank and then prepare for my business mentor appt. He's helping me do biz development into a new area/venue/line of inquiry. Hope it pays off as I have to go into DC to do it. Ugh! Well, that was two poetic quotes/paraphrases.

A bit of drama - We are willing but we are hesitant due to our past experiences - not being proactive and no thank you note from last time. Tends to make any host/hostess hesitant. I will soon be even more ancient, gnarled, and gravely debilitated than before! That is correct, my birthday fast approaches. Reservations have been made and all things party are in the works. So why aren't you couples responding?? Hmmmm?? Chicken? LOL Anyway Ciao, babies!!!!!!!!!!!!

01/31/2006

Why state your preferences up front? Why not let people wander around in the dark? Much better to watch people proposing to people who are patently uninterested. Sexual preferences are irrational and it is pointless to argue against them - I am inordinately fond of 40 yr old teddybears - go figure! I am all for stating your preferences up front - it saves all of us time and energy. I just wish there were more teddybear fanciers out there. He needs more variety in his diet.

More calling today. Shame it is so wet outside. If it were nicer I could go outside and play instead of calling.

The Commonwealth of Virginia continues on its mind boggling way. I have to register as a representative of myself, which costs money, and must furthermore - retake an exam, more money, I already took because they rescinded my previous exam because the time had run out to become a representative of myself. Makes no sense. So I can keep my company and yet cannot do any business - kinda. I also cannot associate with myself since I am an unlicensed person. Now that's going to be difficult! This is all silliness! Time to call the lawyers!

Very soon now, it will be another year that I have escaped the forces of doom and remain here to add grace a man's living room sofa by lounging naked upon it or his bed depending upon which comes first. In celebration, for the next two weeks, I will unbutton shirt buttons of all comely males. The line forms on the left, thank you, nice and orderly now, no pushing. *EG*

How about Strip Duck Duck Goose? Women can only select men and men can only select women. If the tapper reached his/her place, the tappee has to remove an item of clothing before doing his/her rounds. If he/she doesn't reach his/her place before being tagged then the tapper has to remove a piece of clothing before going around again. 4 items of clothing each and minimum of 10 persons in 5 couples. Perhaps I had a twisted childhood? Ciao, babies!!

FEBRUARY
2006

02/01/2006

Okay so you don't like Strip Duck Duck Goose. Then how about Strip Dodgeball played with a large Nerf ball? If you get hit, you lose an article of clothing. Catching the ball is permitted and there's no penalty for that. Be grateful I said Nerf ball, I could have said beanbags.

But there's always Barroom Badminton. If you will recall to mind the opening scenes of the Fry and Laurie Jeeves and Wooster TV series on PBS, you will note the background of the Drones Club where two impeccably dressed men seated in club chairs batted a shuttlecock between them whilst holding drinks. They make it look easy - the reality is quite different. Yes I have tried it! Fortunately our chairs had wheels. The darts players were throwing at right angles to us so our paths crossed often. It was 'interesting'. You may want to stick with bocce'.

I was just checking my purse. Someone owes me $100 and I owe someone else $100 so what do you say we take care of this okay? Perhaps at the Taj this Friday? I have to leave now and get some $$ and some gasoline because it is time for my hair appointment. Ah me! The traveling I get to do! I will say hello to Manassas and Crofton for you!! Ciao, babies!!

Reprinted Here With Permission From the Author

The Albatross Flying Club subsidiary of The Office of Wet Fish

Welcome! Pull up a pew and have a couple of quick ones, which you will definitely need, whilst awaiting your flight. We will be carrying various strontium widgets in the cargo hold during this flight which may smash your baggage but at least it won't get lost. We know where everything is; periodically. The pilot has had a modest amount of aviation training, some flight experience, and is moderately sober but you won't mind that once you've taken in a couple of corpse-raisers yourself, now will you? There's no in-flight service so fuel up now and make yourself comfortable. We think he does have a map. We fly only the oldest aircraft here. There's a real sense of 'heritage' in our planes! These old crates have seen it all since the Great War. Repairs are made using only the finest duct tape so you may have the greatest confidence in their airworthiness! We'll get you there! Tuesday. (And not this Tuesday, neither.) For in flight entertainment we offer involuntary extreme aerobatics guaranteed to keep your interest! For you timid flyers, we promise, really we will, to check the weather beforehand. Come Flying with the Albatross Flying Club for an Experience of a Lifetime!

02/03/2006
The sustained lunacy continues:

Strontium Widgets, Ltd. a subsidiary of The Office of Wet Fish

Welcome to Strontium Widgets, Ltd. Our goal is to provide you with useful information about our widgets which we hope will make it easier for you to do business with us. Strontium Widgets, Ltd. has been serving the world's widget community since April 6th, 2000 BCE. We specialize in the manufacturing, servicing and selling of specialty strontium widgets to discriminating widgeters. Site Introduction At this site, you will find out why our widgets are the only ones that meet the demanding requirements of the widget community today. You'll also find out how best to select, purchase, and how to install and use your new strontium widgets. Contact Us Feel free to browse around this site. If you have comments or questions about our widgets or simply need more information and want to contact us immediately, click on the contact button on any page within this site or call us by phone at 609-555-1212. Thanks for visiting and we look forward to serving you with the best of widgets. Welcome to the Strontium Widgets product information page. We offer a variety of widgets that represent the very best in widget technology. Because our quality control standards are high, we manufacture only the highest caliber widgets. Our goal is always to deliver the best possible widgets. Your satisfaction is always of paramount importance. Below is a short list of the products we sell: Strontium widget A - Tri-lobal widget - $500.00 Strontium widget B - Duodudumal, pentagrammic widget for high stress situations - $1,000.00 Strontium widget C - Chemically and biologically inert square widget - $750.00 OPTIONAL SPECIAL OFFER For a limited time and available only to our Internet Customers, we are offing a special discount, of 29%, on widgets type B. This offer is only good until tomorrow, or possibly next week. All of the items listed above are currently available and can be shipped by motor freight to your location. Standard shipping charges will be applied. For more information or to place an order, please contact us either via email by clicking on the contact button on this page. You may also call us at 609-555-1212 from now to forever.

02/06/2006
And for that $1k you could have had some 200 shares of Coca-Cola and done some serious 'playing'! Silly man! Yes, sex is the drive and act while love is emotion; Pg. 46 of Aunt Agatha's Answers. More about foreplay I see - as if its a virtue for a woman to be 'hard starting'. Relax ladies - it is fun after all! Guys - turn the key and hit the button. Vroom! Engines lit! Either way sex is good. Now if you don't mind, Cat needs to be pounced upon.

I paid my rolling through the stop sign traffic ticket *sigh* Oh! I have to call Frank too.

I have gotten some emails asking (LOL) what is a F%^ widget? Well it is a piece of metal that becomes whatever you need it to be - rather like a metallic stem cell. Got it? Very useful things to have around the house. Assuming you are not allergic to widgets as some people are. And if you thought it couldn't get any sillier, well, you are gravely mistaken *EG*. I have more and yes, I know how to use them! Now, about that pouncing..... Ciao, babies!!

02/06/2006
One of the worst things about football, is all of the whining that takes place.

THE OFFICE of WET FISH

A conglomerate of several companies all controlled by this, our mega-holding company. Please put the top back on the barrel or the fish will get out. To learn more about our family of companies, use the links below. I asked you to put the top back. Now see what you have done? You will have to catch and return all of those fish before I can let you move on. Oh dear. It would seem that you were unfamiliar with aquatic species. Lionfish are poisonous. SUBSIDIARIES: Strontium Widgets, Ltd., The Albatross Flying Club, The Wilston Green Underwater Tatting Society, My Foes Outstretched beneath a tree, Intellectual Honeybunny, Exult, Metallic2, High, Wide and Plentiful.

Further companies will be added as we acquire them. Since we are bent upon global conquest, you may expect us in your neighborhood shortly.

02/07/2006
The best commercial was the Sprint one where the cell phone was used as a crime deterrent. Now THAT was funny! I find football boring in most cases but that 75 yard run to a touchdown was TREMENDOUS - who'da thought such massive beefs could move like that?!?! And another person complaining about how some humans don't remove their body hair - honey, don't complain to us - complain to the manufacturer! Personally I adore fur but then it is about the person not the packaging so long as somewhere close to HWP. Okay what's the next blog about. Share the happiness? You betcha! I agree!! Wheeee!!!

The Muslims have just proven the cartoonist's point. Muslims can 'dish it out' but cannot 'take it'.

Now then - 10 Things About You. A new Blog Run. Tell us 10 Things About You - short one sentence tidbits of information that we may or may not know about you. Since those who start these things should go first, here are mine. Please absolve Cat of any responsibility. 1. I look best either naked or wearing neutral colors. 2. I tend to be head shy. 3. If provoked, will attack rather than hide. 4. I dislike vegetables and prefer beef. 5. I love to drive fast cars fast. 6. I just love to drive anything fast period. 7. Single malt scotch is my drink. 8. I REALLY have this thing for teddybears. 9. Men are both strange and great. 10. I LOVE ROCK N ROLL !!! Ciao, babies!!!

02/08/2006
Hmmm no takers on the '10 Things About Me" run. You cannot ALL be shy - remember, I have read your blogs! So I am not buying into that! I know! Post in one of these clubs and pass out pens and paper. Jeez! Come on peeps! You know I don't go there and that I do nothing in public except flirt like crazy. Well, ahem.. I do periodically try to drag you back to my lair for nefarious sexual purposes, but that's another story. So type them up and post them here where I can see them, please!

Any dommes out there willing to help a 'sister' out?

Attended a VA CPN meeting last night. It was interesting. We met some very nice people. We were warned off discussing politics but oh well! I need some new clothes - mine are looking tired esp my blacks. Did you all enjoy the red dress I wore last Friday? I hope you did because I have two more you will see over the next 4 Fridays. BTW anyone else want to strangle that DJ? LOL Sorry only half kidding! I will try to restrain myself. Oooops! poor choice of words. Ciao, babies!

02/09/2006
Hurray! Thank you! And I agree that being a Dad is tough work but I am sure you are man enough to handle it with style, grace, and good humor. I have found a sense of humor to be essential when dealing with others esp with kids. The slings and arrows of fortune being what they are - outrageous. Note to some: do not spurn me because I am not bi and I won't spurn you for being bi even if the only male you do remains your own husband. Okay, do we have a deal? Cool. No word from the domme's yet.

Word to the wise - Never ever take a hungry man grocery shopping with you. And if your male is a teenager - leave him at home!

The party on the 16th is packed! YES!! I shall need another bottle of champagne I think. Such lovely people! Bring a towel with you and we will see what trouble we can get into in the shower! Well, it is time for me to see if I can interest Cat in doing something or other now. Work, sex, work, sex - the poor man!! LOL Ciao, babies!

02/10/2006
I had damn well better get a gift on St. Valentine's Day !!!!! This year, I am getting an orgy! Wheeee! Flowers, chocolates, a card, and an orgy! What more could a kitten want? Thank you my mildly

166

evil and witty teddybear! Kisses all over you! Yes I know we did that last night. Well, I thought you liked it! Do you mean to tell me that you'd rather have hugs? No? Oh, I must have misunderstood you. I see what it is. You want to have both!! * we interrupt this blog entry* Off to work with you!!!

Remind me to call Frank on Monday morning.

Currently endeavoring to teach culinary skills to the JRM in preparation for his eventually leaving my house and setting up one of his own. Thus far we have done ham, steaks and a turkey. Pies and fruitcakes have also been mastered. Now we will do soups, stews and cookies. After this, it will be sewing as in how to re-affix buttons and patch blue jeans. What one might call The Basic Life Skills for the Single Male. Laundry and cleaning have already been covered. Thank goodness! Else this place would be very messy! Well, off I go! Frolic, frolic, frolic! Ciao, babies!!!!!!!!!!!!

02/12/2006
Next hotel party is in the planning stages. Party is scheduled for Mar 16th beginning at noon. Volunteers are being accepted on the understanding that the Selection Committee will review and choose. Looking for willing HWP males age 30 to 50. 3 to 4 women expected to participate. Cute HWP couples may come if playing separately. One bedroom will be non-smoking. Thank you! BTW this open enrollment period will close on Feb 20th. CatNip

02/13/2006

'A product of public education' used as a pejorative expression is the mark of the extremely ill-bred. Kindly cease and desist. Now then, I have called Frank but since he must take his medications for his various ills and these will have some very strong effects upon him for a time, he will not be able to return my call until this afternoon. We are to have lunch this Friday. As of yet there has been no word on the contract that is supposed to implement this week. I await their call to come and sign. Now to return to my favorite activity - pouncing upon Cat !! Ciao, babies!!!!!!!!!!!!

02/14/2006

Oh dear - seems some people are terribly confused. Squirting - the release of a complex carbohydrate fluid from the Biden glands inside the vagina - means she has not only orgasmed but that she's been blasted past Jupiter and may not have 'come down' from orbit just yet. In other words, it is a good thing! In order to achieve this release, she must be both aroused and relaxed and squirting is, therefore, a testament to the man's skill. Inexperienced persons often find squirting confusing - the women because squirting initially feels like you want to urinate (you aren't) - and the men because no one has ever told them that women do 'ejaculate' also. The fluid, which I am informed tastes sweet, is actually there to maintain the health of the vagina which is almost always having various things inserted into it. It is not a water sport which is a designation solely reserved for other much more 'alternative' activities. In case you are wondering - yes, I do squirt. Got Cat in the eye once! LOL He came up smiling. So we use a lot of towels - it is all good! And no, she will not squirt all of the time or every time. Just relax and enjoy it when she does.

Remember, you can always go and look it up.

Happy Valentine's Day!!!! I recommend playing the Beatle's "All you Need is Love' at the volume level generally known as puree' and drinking copious amounts of expensive champagne while dancing naked in the hot tub. CELEBRATE!!!!

02/15/2006
Interesting that two of the ladies who wrote about their recent discoveries re: squirting received what amounts to 'hate email' and yet the blog entry I posted got only thank you notes from the two ladies involved. Hmm. One fellow with whom we had been conversing on the topic finally broke down and admitted that he had bodily fluid issues in spite of the fact that he expected his wife to accept his sperm however he chose to deliver it. That ended that conversation! Oh, we were diplomatic about it (Cat's doing.) but our thoughts were pretty clear. 4 letter word beginning with a W.

Thanks to all of those people we sent me birthday wishes yesterday. Very sweet of you!! Hugs and Kisses!!

You Know Its Going to be a Bad Playdate When...... 1. she sits on her man's lap and ignores your man's lap. 2. It's been 2 hours and the women haven't cum yet. 3. You can't find anything to say that interests the other couple....Talked to a man who skis now and who used to be the captain of his high school shooting team about the bialathon and got...nothing! No spark! Oookay - guess he's not into me. It happens. Fortunately Cat can discuss super string theory with me so that I don't feel left out. Well, it is time I got wet and then dressed - not the reverse; not yet anyway *w*

Actually , yes you guys do need to be reminded to do something special for your loved one! Hence St. Valentine's Day. Now for you biased persons - just think of it as another excuse to PARTY!!! Kissing the women in honor of Cupid cannot be all THAT bad!! LOL

PLEASE NOTE: the March 16th party has been changed to the 9th. Please review and let me know if you can still cum!!!

02/16/2006
Please be it noted that if you RSVP yes and then do not show, well, just do not ask us if you can come the next time. You might find the answer hard to take. Both Miss Manners and Emily Post are very clear and very firm on this topic. Only being diseased, being in the hospital due to a horrible accident or your death excuses your absence. Of course, if the police arrest you and throw you in jail, you do get one phone call - have your lawyer call us with your regrets. BTW you missed one GREAT party!!!

It is with deep sorrow that I have to tell you, Frank did not come through.........yet. Still waiting!!

So I have a weekend free to hang about with my darling. We have a bit of gardening to do. I can

170

continue work on my book and do some housecleaning. We do have to do a wardrobe review and note who needs what. All of this in preparation for the polo season when we will not have time for very much. If 'someone' would give permission, help is available for stump removal and deck building! Perhaps Sunday? Power tools and 3 inch deck screws provided free of charge. We have leftovers. Anyway, now that I have vented my ire, I suppose I will retreat to my hot tub and finish off the leftover champagne!! Ciao, babies!!!

02/17/2006

Since Frank has fallen through and I am NOT driving up to Aberdeen today, I will go to the farm, not The Farm, and pick up my hind 1/4 of cow they have for me. $400 for 4 months of meat. Once the boy leaves, that $400 of meat will last 6 months! How cool is that? And if you like liver, they'll give it to you for free. I suppose if you're making Pepper Pot soup they'll also give you some tripe for free. Of a skull with horns for you O'Keefe or southwest decor lovers. One only has to ask.

The Office of Wet Fish Speaks!
President & CEO - CURRENTLY TESTIFYING BEFORE THE SENATE SUBCOMMITTEE on THE THREAT TO PUBLIC HEALTH re: STRONTIUM WIDGETS
Production - Efficiency combined with effectiveness is the key to profitable production. To this end, you are all now being replaced with machines. Thank you.
The Moneymen - DEWEY, CHEATEM & HOWE
A combined financial and legal firm, we specialize in being all things to all men for maximum

171

profitability to us. We act as inside accountants and outside auditors as well as the legal advisors and all to the same firm. How cool is that? Time being relative, there is no reason not to charge in 15 minute increments. Your time is up. That will be $1,000,006.00. Thank you.

Shipping Department - SCHEDULES PROCEEDING ACCORDING TO PLAN DELIVERY EXPECTED TUESDAY BUT NOT THIS TUESDAY

Human Resources - Since you have all been replaced by machines, here is your pink slip...... and to spare you the problem of rolling over your pensions, we have stolen them. We feel your pain. Thank you. NEXT!

Ciao, babies!!!

02/19/2006
Spent the day looking at houses thinking...a king bed would fit here...I'd put a queen sized bed right here....oh and over there I could slip in a twin bed. Guess 'entertaining' was on my mind huh?

02/20/2006
Its cleaning the office day. This means shoveling my way through papers of all kinds, filing the books back onto the shelves (alphabetized by author's last name) and generally attempting to quell the chaos. Then the dusting and vacuuming can begin. Days off are hardly ever days off for me. Cat had a very nice weekend but I will just let your imaginations handle that one. He will have more fun later on this week as well as another free weekend. Whoot! - as my son would say.

I will have to call (and harass?) Frank a lot this week - but then, he deserves it!

Men also have this habit of leaving their watches on. Socks and watches! The one scrapes your skin while the others make you want to laugh at them! Can you say DORK? So guys, much as I love you - please, naked means naked! Take it ALL off! (remember that commercial?) Ok enough fun and frivolity! Off to the fray! Ciao, babies!!!

02/21/2006
OMG yesterday I found my desk! I knew it was in there - had to be- papers don't just levitate. Yes, there is actual wood, no not that kind, showing! Now to do the bills - irk! Yes, well. It had to happen. I always feel sad when those dollars sprout wings and fly away like that! FINALLY I get my cruise control back on my Expedition. Yippee skippy! But I had to call them and ask if they had it - they didn't call me. I know who you are and what you drive, he told me - then why didn't you call me?

Harass Frank. Harass Frank. Harass Frank

OK lingerie is sexy but when you have 14 men to do in 4 hours, it just gets in the way. Cute earrings and a bit of perfume is my usual play attire. Cat is in charge of collecting all 'lost' earrings because by the time I am through, I get all purry and giggly which amuses Cat and gives him the chance to be all male protective. Trust me ladies, once a man gets it into his head that you are 'cute' there's no going back. I want to be bewitching and beguiling but all I get is 'cute'. I am so doomed! Doomed to be 'cute' from now on. If Smokey says 'gravity' once more, I may ignore his recent surgery and tickle him vigorously. Ciao, babies!!!

02/22/2006
My oh my - some people have been nipping on the ire juice this morning! Short answers to each topic: 1. execute him already, 2. not necessary to make them glow the Sunnis have just exploded a Shiite mosque - the Shiites will take care of them now. 3. do NOT sell the ports, and 4. stop the Patriot Act - its just your paranoia talking and do you really want to portray yourself as a timid mouse? Just don't get me started.

Did you remind me about my having to harass Frank???

It was Boys Night Out last night and WOW does he get giggly when he's lit!! Had fun teasing the hell out of him when he got back. Can I undo your shirt buttons, Mister? Tee heeee! Oh, oh! He's smoldering at me! This is where I scamper off to bed! Ciao, babies!!

02/23/2006
For our morning convocation, "That I Would be Good" by Alanis Morissette. Serenity, serenity, serenity. You can have a beer after work. Do you think three coats of nail polish are enough? I ask because tonight I and then we have an appt. Hmmm I also have to print out my spreadsheet for the CPA. Get all of that to her. It is time to pay Uncle Sam. Have to make sure I have all of my papers in order. There is that very EZ 1040 Form. You know, the one where it asks how much you made last year and then says 'send it to us'?

174

The Selection Committee for March's party is meeting even as we speak. Invitations will be sent out March 1st.

What else is on the agenda? Grocery getting. Now that the cruise control on the Expedition has been re-done, the truck performs much better. Apparently its computer cannot handle not having that circuit operative. Twas sluggish. You know how women hate sluggishness. This particular woman hates financial columnists getting their facts wrong as in this idea that financial planners do not have any qualifications since they aren't required. HAH! A quick look at the NASD website would soon disabuse her of that idea! In order to do what I do, she would need a Series 65 which you cannot get until after you have gotten a Series 7. For more information just ask and I will send you some exam questions. Then you may want to go and lie down. Like I wish I could put on my voicemail: "If you'd like to panic because the market dropped several points, press 5 and scream into the phone." Ciao, babies!

02/24/2006
It is interesting how goals direct behavior. His goal is variety. Hers is supplementary. He wants to expand his sexual experience and is therefore oriented toward having sex with many women. Her experience being already wide and deep, she's looking for something rather more. Those with whom he has formed relationships will not be precisely slighted but they will have a lower priority with him than a new woman or perhaps even work he's brought home from the office. It depends upon

the individual situation, of course, but that's the general impression. She is much more likely to ignore the work she brought home from the office until after the fun and games. Her priorities are enjoy her usual men first then the work and then perhaps a new man or two. Excepting parties, of course. But then, sometimes fantasies are best left just being fantasies.

I have been credibly informed that come the summer, I will be a grandmother. YES!!! Will I have to change my ways or will I become, as Cat has said, a GILF? Will I have to give up my body surfing whilst wearing my micro-thong bikini? In any case, come June/July there will be a road trip! How many stuffed animals is considered 'too many'? Warning: I will have pix!!

Called Frank...again.

Shoe addiction??? Jeez! Buy some shares of stock instead! Or bonds. Or pork bellies! Or companies ripe for a hostile takeover! Yeah, shoes are great but, lets face it, they aren't The Rush!! 7 inch heels??? Is this anything like guys wanting to jack up their trucks so they can put 35 inch rims and tires on them? *shaking head sadly* I'd much rather be that tigress a man barely glimpses out of the corner of his eye via a patch of rippling stripes dimly seen at the edge of light from the campfire. Not a stripper but a succubus. Ciao, babies

02/25/2006
The Ultimate Winter Bed

guaranteed to keep even the tenderest of ladies warm and comfortable through the night

begin with a firm, if not rock hard, mattress and box springs then cover this with a 2 to 3 inch featherbed. use 600 thread count sheets - yes, a bit pricey but the will last almost to forever so its worth it on go the sheets in the usual approved manner (if you don't know - ask). if your budget cannot stand 600 thread count sheets - you may use flannel sheets on top of this, place what is known as a mink blanket that is to say a double thickness heavy weight blanket. (this will help mold the fabrics to her body preventing cold air infiltration) top off with a down comforter in a flannel cover; yes the heavy blanket goes under the comforter. Three firmnesses of pillows are best: rock hard, medium and squishy all in 600 thread count or flannel pillow slips. You may use less if you don't have a king size bed. Why don't you have a king size bed btw? Nevermind.

To make it very special indeed, add one attractive and congenial adult male human.

02/27/2006
I am not willing to travel any distance at all to attend an on premises club - permit me to explain - too far away, too many $$, too much socializing, not enough action. If Cat doesn't get to play then neither do I. Got it? Good. NEXT TOPIC. I wouldn't mind Republicans so much if they kept their noses out of what doesn't concern them i.e. who marries whom and what's in a woman's womb. None of their business. How many of you here are promoting abstinence?

Frank is not well.

I have a few phone calls to make. So I'll let you go now. Ciao, babies!

02/28/2006
Yes Mark of Alley writes a wonderful book but I use Miss Manners. Answer the email - it won't kill you. And if you found the time to read it - you have the time to answer it. Just write yes, no or eeeeek!!! as applicable. Next - screen names- we chose Catnip because that's his effect upon me and I am somewhat feline in personality. Also I bite hence I am Nip and he is Cat. He is also furry - just how I like men to be. I have yet to see another with the same, and it swings with our real names anyway so - it works. Mmmmmmmeow!

No nibbling Nip's nips now!

The Commonwealth of VA's SCC is coming to audit me on Monday so I am somewhat fraught at this moment so please excuse anything didactic. I have to gather and tabulate, arrange or otherwise make sense of all of my business formation materials. Good thing I cleaned up my office last weekend! Develop a privacy policy to satisfy the Gramm-Leach-Bliley Act and I also have to get all of the filing done. Eeeeeeeeeeeek!!! No stress in my life! HAH!! So if you see someone running off screaming into the night - don't worry - its just me. Ciao, babies!!

MARCH
2006

03/01/2006

Okay the invitations to THE Social Event of March are now out. Thank you for volunteering! Hope you can come! If you do not know the rules, please ask. Should be a GREAT party!

Being audited by the Commonwealth of VA's SCC this coming Monday so forgive me for being anxious. I am not sleeping well.

So on to the next thing on the list. Ciao, babies!

03/02/2006

Lent? Oh! Lent! I see. Give up something you enjoy for a time? Why would I do that? What is the point? Are you sure? Isn't that rather atavistic? Moderation would seem to be more the thing really. But if you want to participate go right ahead. Not me though. I am too busy franticly running around in ever decreasing circles.

4 days til audit.

Favorite movie? CASABLANCA -was there ever any doubt? I am a fan of Bogart. I also like Hepburn and Grant. TOPPER was also a good flick and THE THIN MAN is also very funny. Monty Python is excellent as are Jeeves and Wooster. But I do not spend a lot of time with movies and TV. Well, back to my stressing! Ciao, babies!

03/03/2006

Oookay so we are to meet some people tonight and if we can latch on or pick up an additional male that would be nice. This could get very interesting! (note the German accent) What "Let's Fuck" email??

Look people, we are the ones almost guaranteed to fuck you silly and yet you don't send us email?!??! Or is that it? You don't want to give us ideas. No provoking the kitten? Tsk, tsk.

3 days until the audit - I would like to thank Smokey for helping me out with my prep! KISSES SMOKEY!!

Party attrition has set in - this time amongst the women. We need an attractive woman who is seriously in sex with men - who feels that if one man is good, 12 is better - think of it as a masculine buffet - a little of him and some of him and I'll try a bit of that guy over there. You do not have to dress up or go to the work of building a relationship - all you have to do is whistle. How cool is that? A man without all of the work and then he goes home afterwards and there's no fuss! Multiplied. Time for me to go! I am picking up Smokey....again *w* Ciao, babies!!!

03/06/2006
In the dark, I stand next to you at first and then put my arm around you and breathe on your neck murmuring something to your earlobe. Close your eyes and imagine what sex with me would be like. My hand in your hair forces you to tilt your head back and I kiss your throat before lightly teasing your lips with the tip of my tongue- perhaps I will kiss you – very, very lightly and fleetingly. A kiss from a wraith. Claws run slowly and lightly down your spine. Love biting the nape of your neck. Nothing about you is sacred. I will enjoy every inch of your body but so slowly, ever so slowly. Savoring. There in the dark.

182

In the dark, I crouch above your prostrate naked body feeling your warmth. Feeling the texture of your skin beneath my cheek as I caress you with my lips, the top of my knee resting snuggly up against your testicles. Lick a spot and then breathe on it. How would it feel getting this close to me? Claws run slowly and lightly up along the side of your hip. There is no escape for you now. There is no rest for you now. Each orgasm you have will only make you more vulnerable for the next. You have no limits with me. My skin sliding along your skin and fur. My hands, lips and body reveling in yours. Hard, soft, pleasure, pain its all there; in the dark.

In the dark, I seek your total disintegration to orgasmic sensory overload. I want you to quiver in both fear and delight. Once. To lose all vestige of control from anticipation alone. Cum for me; then cum again, and again, and again. Feel me alongside of you. Twice. Feel me around you. Slow, relentless, rhythmic. Timed to the beating of your heart. Will you resist? Can you resist? My lips on yours. My juices all over you. The long slow sliding into oblivion. Thrice. Sucking your fingers, you nipples, your penis. Feeding from you. Hair thin red lines sloping around your waist gently licked. Before I leave you, in the dark.

03/07/2006
OKAY the Commonwealth of VA's SCC came, asked, looked, and went. Now awaiting the bad news in an official letter. They didn't haul me off to court so I might be okay. We shall see. But the stressing is now over. BTW Thanks to Smokey there for helping me out even though he doesn't like

my driving (grrrr) as he did last Thurs/Fri. My office now looks GREAT!

so you didn't enjoy my prose piece???

Music to have sex by?? Excuse me but do people do that? Look y'all perhaps Cat's spoiled here but a strong breeze can make me cum so music, soft lighting, scented oils may be nice but usually he's far too busy just trying to keep up to deploy all of that. But we did pause long enough for me to ask him what his HOT BUTTONS were and he was at a loss for words. Then he explained that most guys have to spend so much energy just getting a woman into bed and then doing all they can to keep her there that they haven't any energy left for cataloging their own HOT BUTTONS. Being a purrrrry sort, I immediately set about exploring. *EG* Yes, Cat has HOT BUTTONS. Now to go and press a few of them! Ciao, babies!

03/09/2006
Thursday was more interesting and some of you did get to see me in my suit (the same one) which makes me look oh so professional and very biz like. But this time - I attended a 'Stress Management Seminar' or 'Group Therapy' as we like to call it. *EG* Once again, those men with 'standing invitations' proved their worth DAMN WHAT A GREAT TIME!! Two soaked beds!! Both ladies enjoyed themselves to the fullest!! Thank you - you wonderful men - all of you! Aaaah!

03/10/2006
Mmmmmmmmeow! Still afterglowing!! I do so enjoy group therapy. Fortunately, so do most men. In

184

addition to this Frank called me. What a first! Yeeehaw - so very soon now fun, fun, fun!! Baby! Baby! I have to disagree in part - they'd know what to do with them - what they wouldn't remember would be who you were. Just think! Perpetual first dates!!! As for the age thing - while he doesn't object to say 25 on up, I find men younger than 40, on average, far too obtuse for me.

Yes there was another blacklist with this party - People if you aren't into it, do not sign up for it - don't lie - Yes, you guessed it - said they were out of town for the entire week and then 'lo and behold' posted a playtime note "come and fuck with us at our house tonight" the day before the party. Might hold a party just for those special 6 men who have 'standing invitations'.

Just another quiet weekend this weekend. Grocery getting again , then picking up some battery cables and perhaps something outside if the weather holds. Come On, Sun!!!! Next week is a slew of conference calls and getting my hair done and other sundries before the Taj and a house party. Off to find some molasses! Ciao, babies!!!

03/13/2006
It is all about the garden. 3 plants = $300.00 ah well! Some large plants did not survive the winter so we dug them up and went off to price replacements. You know how it is when I get into a nursery - Oooo these are nice! Hence the bill. You buy stripper shoes; I buy rhododendrons, and battery cables as the MGB decided it was time, dammit, so get thee to the Otter Parts.

New pix possible Wednesday but we will see.

April's party is going to be the Cat Toy Appreciation Party - 6 men and 12 women; the men already know who they are - now we just need SERIOUS, cute, and kinda hwp women to overwhelm their senses and make them forget their names! Two ladies thus far with another three flirting with the idea - two of whom will be ditching the 'old man' for the afternoon. I am sure they will tell them all about it later. Ciao, babies

03/14/2006
But that would mean that we only see those blogs extolling the events and not hearing from those for whom the event was less than an event. Yes they sound like large M&Gs but apparently some did not know about the open door play upstairs. In any case, we do not go to these things but I do believe both sides should be heard.

Does not look like new pix will be forthcoming. Sorry.

Few truly adventurous women apparently. Tsk, tsk, tsk. What? Do I have to get in a stock of beads? LOL I am hoping the lady from Boston can fly down for this party. The guys really like her. Hmmmm who else? *checking Rolodex* Ah, yes!! And she's already gotten the next three party dates off - specifically so she can attend. Nice lady! Yes I know the party's more than a month away but I PLAN these things. With the correct planning all difficulties can be over-come. I shall find sufficient ladies who have the 'ovaries' for this sort of thing! *EG*

186

Okay new pix and...

Oooo you think I am going to steal your man away do you?? HAH!!! BTW - when did you want him back? *has daytimer open and ready* Okay, after he's done being passed around, I will return him to you ... let's say next Tuesday at 9pm? That work for you? Or won't your lover be out of the house by then?

If these events were huge orgies instead of just huge M&Gs I would actually attend one! or two...um...okay I'd go to ALL of them! But playing silly games, doing displays of my flesh, collecting beads - just not me, hun. Going by the estimate of 800 people I will assume, some singles, so lets cut that down to 700 half of which would be women so that makes it 350 males. Half of them, going by my past success rate, would not be interested in me so that leaves me with 175 men to be getting on with. But since my sweety would not be enjoying 175 women - does he just wish!- it is not going to happen. Fair is fair.

03/15/2006

We have time constraints so if the play doesn't start as soon as we walk in the door- we are out of there! Certain persons know this and they have someone lying in wait for me. We also host parties where any socializing and hanging out is done during rest periods. Boundaries? Guys have boundaries? imagine that! LOL Themes?? Is this the prom? The theme is sex - always. Okay maybe a birthday *w* but sex should come into this too. I am not driving for hours, invariably getting lost on the way, if I am not getting anything from the guys. Pay close attention to your guest list making sure there is someone for everyone to play with and your party should be a BLAST!

So there you have it! Ashanti's laid back party and Nip's why are you still wearing clothes party. *chuckling*

There is a house party coming up. You know what that means. I get to have fun! All of those willing men! Actually, willing or not, they are coming into my bed. Or that bed over there. *EG* I do hope they are prepared. I can get quite testy if I have to wait. I especially like it if the men volunteer. Let's see...how many, going head to tail as it were, can we get into a chain? Ladies above, men below- Hmmmm I am purring already!

Ladies, if you were curious about getting into groups but were nervous, this next party is very female-friendly. Twice as many women as men (please note: the men have already been selected) and quite frankly we are imperfect too and not as young as we once were. HWP and serious about playing/toying with men is all we are asking. Kindly consult your calendars and sign up!

03/16/2006
If you are still using scrunchies, you need to get your hair over to a really good hairdresser and say 'take care of this'. Long hair - been there done that - no more and it used to be below my shoulder blades. You have seen the pix. Now I have a jazzy, rich bitch haircut that's towel dry and go. Way more kewl and I can get out of his house faster afterwards. *EG*

webcasts this afternoon! WTF? Her oral duties?!?! What is UP with you? Duties indeed! HAH! Feeding off the male for once is more like it! Give it up, fellows! LOL And if you have to tie your hair back - PFFFT Neophytes! BAN SCRUCHIES!! *dancing gleefully around the fire* BURN SCRUNCHIES!!

Polo starts this year May 27th at 7pm. Yeeehaw! This is how it works, polo from 7 to say 10 Friday and Saturday then off to party! Change in the truck on the way back or you all will just have to deal with my jeans or the polo crowd will have to deal with skimpy summer dresses and sandals. I will start working on my tan in April - I think. Going to PA to do a roof in April which is our family's version of a reunion. WORK PARTY! Uncle and aunt will be flying up for this. His third wife now. Be nice to meet her. Lots to do! (This includes doing Cat) Ciao, babies!!

03/17/2006
Green huh? Well, to be quite truthful, I should be wearing both the green and the orange. "they all began to fight. And me being strictly neutral, I bashed everyone in sight." Hey, its a party of sorts. But it will mean digging through my closets to see what I have - one would think that someone as organized as I usually am would have something at the ready - but this is not the case. Anyone up for a little James Joyce? Do not play "When Irish Eyes are Smiling" either - new words to that song! *EG*

I do not drink beer, stout, ale - etc. No hops please. This is a hop free zone. Let's talk Irish whiskey instead.

Celtic traditions being what they are, some lady should come dressed in all black with feathers, another lady in leathers and we should have one strong, pure and true high soprano soaring above the instruments in a whirling melodic line. T'would be a mighty party! But as for me: once a MacDonald (Scots) married a Patterson (Irish) whose offspring then got involved matrimonially with an Allen (Welsh) it was all over! The P Celts and the Q Celts became one - and here we are today. "And you made me the Thief of Your Heart." Slainte' !!!!!!!!

03/19/2006
Party, Party, Party !!!

Had a WONDERFUL time at the party last night!! All of those delicious men - and all of them available! Aaaaaaaaaaaaaah! So if you hear me breaking out into spontaneous giggles - now you will know why. *EG*

Thank you!!!

03/20/2006
Two play dates and one training session this week in addition to the studying and other sundry course work. Everyone likes my blogs but they never run with them. If I were a person with delicate and tender sensibilities, I would be wounded but as I haven't...ah well... you all are safe. Perhaps I will develop some as time goes on. You never know. It

190

could happen. Stop laughing at the idea! Jeez! Oooo just you wait until you are in my reach! You will pay.

BTW if we've played with you at parties are you SURE you wouldn't like to get together outside of parties? Hmmmm?

Well I guess you all know yourselves best but why on earth would a woman hold back from having an orgasm beats me. I like to have as many, of any size, as is possible! 30, 40 more- any number! Just keep them coming! I esp enjoy those rolling orgasms that just go on and on forever! Wheeeeeeeeeeeeeee! So blast me past Jupiter baby, I love it! BTW, yes Virginia, the topic did come up in casual conversation.

Songs from high school? I was not in high school in the 80's. I graduated from Penn State in 1977 and then went into the US military. I was in Korea in 80-81 and then in what was then West Germany and then at Scott AFB in Illinois. At that time I was listening to Corelli and Cherubini and Vivaldi. A little Bach and a lot of Beethoven at the setting known as puree' - I love loud music! Besides, what is your hang up with high school? College was and remains a LOT more fun!! Ciao, babies!!

03/21/2006
Bringing you up to date on various topics: 1.Hmmm not good. Seems my trainee really failed his test. TSK, TSK. Some increased hands-on training will now begin. This is gonna hurt...............him! 2. Cat is available whenever you want him but I am only available by prior arrangement. Give me a heads up

the day before. 3. I have to call Frank. 4. exam date is 31 March at noon. 5. The poll results are in: people want me rapacious and wearing black and if we were sharing a guy and you had unprotected sex with him - you SHOULD tell me who he was because condoms can break and if he had unprotected sex with you, he most likely also had it with others.

No answers to why a woman would hold back from having an orgasm.

One month out and only one adventurous woman has come forward! What's up with that? You know it is going to be an amazing party! Let your appetite loose! Ditch the 'old man' and come on out! Send me an email and we will put you onto the guest list. Easy peasy. We hold parties once per month and this one is going to be one of the more interesting ones but for it to happen we need some suitable women. What's suitable? hwp, mischievous, cute, loves to have sex with men. Ciao, babies!

03/22/2006
I have been a bad, bad kitten *EG* but it was so much FUN that I am sure he and Cat didn't mind. MMMM scented oils. OH! Sorry! went into a daydream there for a moment. My past coming out? That would shock even you all! LOL Sssshh! don't tell anyone. I am trying to be sociable but it is so difficult when the guys want to spank me. My reaction to being spanked is not positive. *kindly notice the evil gleam in my eyes* Hissss, spit, spit!

you really must read Skippy's List

2 women thinking about it and 2 women have signed up for April's party. I have the brie, crackers and wine ready for polo on May 27th. May's party on the 22nd btw is an open call one. Let's see...what else is on the list.. more new pix that's next week, have to buy a new truck and renovate the bathrooms here. Wonder if I should get the bickering gay couple to help out there. Hmmm. 2 gays guys = 1 woman when it comes to decor? Possibly. 3 new plants to go in later this month. My exams. an MFM when the guys can get their schedules to mesh. BUSY, BUSY - but we can fit you in *W* Ciao, babies!!

03/23/2006
"Just one chance Just one breath Just in case there's just one left"

I hope not, I love fur - on men. I have often remarked that I have this thing - a SERIOUS attraction- to 40 year old and 6 ft teddybears. MMMMMMMMMMmmmmmmmm. Oh dear! Day lusting again! Sorry. A man simply has to have fur to qualify as a teddybear. All of you going eeewww would most likely rather stroke a shaved cat instead of a nice furry one - yeah. Right. Try just running your hands over the tips of his fur - real ghosting - and see his reaction. Very tantalizing experience for him!

Will they, wont' they; will they, won't they; won't they join the dance?

Jealousy is a learned response and it can be unlearned - stop thinking of him/her as YOURS but rather as a person in his/her own right albeit one who is very special to you. Those who are jealous are insecure somewhere in that relationship and the only to get over it is to face up to your fears. Will whatever you fear kill you? No? Then it doesn't really matter now does it? It may hurt but that will not last. I may end up single again. if so, none of you men will be safe!! Bwahahahahaa! Ciao, babies!

03/24/2006

"I love the way you respond to caresses; being touched by my hands and lips. Up along your arms, over you shoulders, sliding across your jaw and cheek, down your back, and over your thighs and rump, finishing with the lightest of lingering kisses on your lips. I give as good as I get and I want your body, blood and your very soul to sing with passion."

You do know I arrange parties in conjunction with another friend of mine don't you? Attention single men! Well I have been asked to find young hardbody ethnic guys who play well amidst others for a party in Bethesda during the day on April 7th. I am asking all those who meet the criteria to volunteer. First name, cell and pix please. How many times have you heard that, single guys? Apparently this one is going to be 3 women and however many men. Hmm. Could be fun! I might have to take my vitamins! *EG* Ciao, babies!

03/27/2006

Lets review: movies of seduction, training films, pornography, art films. Quite so. Not ever to be compared with the real thing. Besides who has the time?? There are so many men out there that I despair - so little time! Writing shopping list for next party: blindfolds, chocolate sauce, scented body oils for massages, extra towels. 12 women have 6 men in their sights for this one. The plan is to find out how much stimulation they can take. Dontcha love it when I get 'experimental'? am supposed to have lunch tomorrow with Frank! The call for single ethnic men has netted me 1, just 1 man! What is wrong? Are they booked? Not interested? Is it something I said?? Don't make me get out my trank dart gun! *image of Nip tranking guys, tying them up and putting them into the back of her huge SUV* a hunting we will go - a hunting we will go - hi ho the merry o - a hunting we will go! The things I do for my friends! Ciao, babies!!!

03/27/2006
Being bitchy for ANY reason counts as DRAMA. So fix it already, dammit!! It happens every month - think you'd either take care of it or fix it by now. JEEZ!

painted the entire interior of my house in three weekends - no mess, no fuss, no drama - and he laughed because I wore my painting clothes - so old the pants kept falling down since the elastic is about gone. Being repeatedly flashed helps any man's mood. Btw do not paint the cat - she doesn't like it.

03/28/2006
Hurray - but I'd tend to blast the guy that says nasty things about her behind her back - what's his issue? It is just sex among friends, guy - get over it. Okay but if you don't want to know, be careful not to ask. They might have their reasons. I agree and, frankly, you cause me great concern. "There's something not

quite right about that boy." Very scary. No, I don't remember the 70's. And the 80's, well, I was out of the States at the time, sorry - wasn't keeping up with the fads. You all visit Europe, I used to live there. Oookay, fine. Well, that seems to be the blogs. BTW I don't get periods anymore but even when I did, I was pretty much the same rapacious and slightly irascible person you see before you now.

twin V-12 engines always idling - just in case

6 men, 8 women and 1 hotel suite = and we'll have fun, fun, fun, you all know the tune. We still need another 4 adventurous cute women - we have 2 of the men not being overwhelmed. Come on ladies! It is fun to see them gasping for air, crying no, no as you drag them back to bed! The men have promised me that they will not put up too much of a fight, that they have been taking their vitamins, and that they will get plenty of rest beforehand. Now to go and 'exercise' Cat. Ciao, babies!!!

03/29/2006
K's Starving Artist Trail Mix

Pistachios, walnuts, almonds, peanuts, pignoli or pine nuts, sunflower seeds apricots, papaya, mango, pineapple, golden raisins, raisins, cherries, cranberries, dates, figs

1 cup each all fruits dried and chopped, all nuts shelled cleaned and pieced. Mix ingredients dry then package in quart sized ziplock bags.

03/29/2006
The Wicked Woman Day Spa for Men

The following package is available for select men.

1. a nice romp in the bed 2. shave 3. facial mask using volcanic mud 4. hair trimming - various areas 5. shoulder massage with scented oil 6. hot shower being vigorous scrubbed down using scented body wash - everywhere 7. dried with warm towels 8. anointed with scented oils - select areas 9. fellatio 10. wrapped in a warm robe and given a scotch and a cigarette and laid on a sofa and fed grapes.

This weekly treatment is esp recommended for stressed-out teddybears.

03/30/2006
Praise in public, castigate in private. - on to more important matters: to wit I have been informed that a session at The Wicked Woman Day Spa for Men is:
vvvvveeeerrrryyyy rrreeeeellllaaaaxxxxiiiinnnnggg.

ROTBL The teddybears are purring even now. Perhaps now would be the time to tell him I am wearing my leathers to the Taj this Friday?

We are still seeking adventurous hwp women for the April 20th party. Remember our motto: Tormenting males is fun!

Exam day is tomorrow so wish me the best of luck! There's a lot riding on this one! I passed the practice test yesterday so all might be well but a little extra luck - a few more brain cells? - never goes amiss. Fortunately there aren't any formulas in this one. *sigh* It is my opinion that ALL formulas should be as simple as $e=mc2$ or $f=m/a$. Either that or they provide computer programs so one enters the data and presses the button. ZAP! Just as it is really done in the real world. Ah me! Time to go and check out the hot tub! Ciao, babies!!!

03/31/2006
Exam Day! Everyone wish me luck, good fortune, and extra brain cells!! Today at noon we will see if this lady still has her profession. This means the Taj tonight will either witness great triumph or great tragedy. In either case, I am wearing my leathers as it makes a great contrast to the gossamer fluffy stuff the other ladies wear - skanky stripper shoes indeed! - or half wear as the case may be. Unfortunately this is a computer run test so there's no chance of intimidating the exam official into giving me a perfect score or near offer.

They were banned? Good Lord! We liked them! They were communicative, bright, and sparkly. Were any reasons given?

I really, really, really, really, want that truck! This means that within the next 6 months I will get a brand new, sorry Cat, Land Rover LR3 HSE model with everything included - for cash. Buying new for three reasons: taxes, special buying options, and I do not want to be out in the back of beyond with inherited vehicle problems. You all should know how I drive by now so a used truck just will not do. I am only willing to put up with vehicular back-talk from classic cars. The MGB is scheduled to go in for major engine work this summer too. Hopefully Cat will not have to be my Knight in Shining Yukon again on the way to the shop. There's something special about a man who will drop everything to

bring you engine oil! KISSES DARLING! Ciao,
babies!!!

APRIL
2006

04/01/2006
Don't you remember when you had your first beer?

04/02/2006
Personally I adore those 'who cares' blogs - reminds me of similar statements that end 'so long as it wasn't me/us' Sound familiar?

This really cute and sexy teddybear and I went out looking at Land Rover LR3's yesterday. The only time the salesman missed a beat is when I asked him its zero to 60 time. That he didn't know. I guess it hadn't come up before. I sooo wanted to try it out during the test ride but my teddybear was cautioning me to play it cool. We did consider testing out its cargo room *EG* yes, you have the correct idea! But the teddybear felt it would be too confining. But I have done a 6'4" male in a VW Beetle before so I am sure something could be worked out! So while he and the manager worked out the numbers - can I have a 10% discount for paying cash?- he, the teddybear, and I drooled over some Jaguars and strolled about looking at cars he might afford - someday. Then I took him back to his place and the inevitable happened!! WHEEEE!!! (reprinted here by popular demand).

In Clinton, Oklahoma, molesting an automobile is illegal.

04/03/2006
The April parties are closed to all but women at this point. May will be an open call party.

I adore fur! So soft, so silky, I just have to pet and nuzzle guys who have fur. I cannot help myself.

Guys who shave below the neck are too naked and not in a good way. Makes them seem prepubescent. I have to throw them back as being too young. Neatly trimmed to approx 1/2 inch is perfect. (I will hand out rulers later.) As to facial hair, I like them nicely trimmed too. Clean shaven is also okay. Having a beard like ZZTop is not okay. Someone I know is at his most attractive sitting adjacent to me in his dining room wearing his bathrobe half open afterwards. I can see his fur and his expression. Mmmmmmmmeow! I have to go and straddle him, facing him, and kiss him. Mmmmmm.

Excuse me. Ah! yes I am blogging! I remember now! Sorry about that! Ahem! So guys please do not shave below the neck. Thank you. Ciao, babies!!!

04/04/2006
If your entire criteria for selecting playmates is based solely upon the physical you will surely live a very unfulfilled life. The content of your character is what counts. Along with wit, charm, inner joy, passion, and compassion - these things matter much, much more than your waistline even in this sexual arena. How many times have I said it? IT IS THE PERSON NOT THE PACKAGING THAT MATTERS. As proof of this statement, I offer into evidence, 'Pleaser'; who doesn't.

from Skippy's List:
Inflatable sheep do *not* need to be displayed during a room inspection.   and
The proper way to report to my Commander is "Specialist Schwarz, reporting as ordered, Sir" not "You can't prove a thing!"

I prefer to see my men wearing one, just the one black leather wrist band around his left wrist and nothing else. I also think I look best when wearing dangling earrings, scented body oil and stiletto high heels and nothing else. Perhaps if we still went to clubs, we could test these 'outfits' out but as it is.... LOL Mmmmmm yes. Ciao, babies!!

04/05/2006
The latitude implicit in "HWP" , generally meaning taller than you are wide, removes from the term any offense. For us, you might find it a 'loaded term' of course. One lady of our 'acquaintance' thinks it means average build or within 10 lb.s of one's ideal weight. But that is my point - that the term HWP can mean whatever you choose it to mean. For me it means anything beyond 'teddybear' is too much, and if you disappear when you turn sideways that's too little. No walking skeletons please. Other than that please be BAP, brain-age proportionate, and stop all of this high school stuff. Thank you.

I would have no problems with American Idol if they would stop pre-empting HOUSE for it!

Well it is time for me to pick up the average American woman's burden of work, family, and house all at the same time! Since someone stayed out late, I have to be quiet. LOL Yes, but it will let me get on without interference for once. *EG* Ciao, babies!

04/06/2006
The sun is up, the sky is bright, and the hot tub is burbling away enticingly what is THAT noise?

Ambersandy! What are you doing girl? Stop that! Jeez! No you cannot merow or meow or make other squeaky brakes noises and expect to avert peril. Cats!! Not to be confused with Cat. Well, the person who drug himself home at 7 ak emma did have an amusing story to tell. I ,naturally, got to hear all about it. You are just going to have to speculate. Accidents and sex were NOT involved. Alcohol was.

She has a Labrador that weighs 110 lbs.? Is she trying to kill the poor dog with food? That is one fat Lab!

Sorry but I have to skip the Taj Fridays for the next three weeks. Us self-employed professionals have to work when we can and then I have a family thing. So I won't be back to the Taj until the 28th. Cat will be around here and there doing the 'social butterfly' thing so you do not forget us in the meantime. OK so he's not particularly 'butterfly-like'. More of a 'social teddybear' thing then? BTW his drink is a Jack and Coke tall. Thank you for your cooperation *W* Ciao, babies!!!

04/07/2006
Got the new battery and a new battery cable into the MGB so we will see if that fixes the problem but not today as it is raining. We sooo love Lucas Electrics, inventors of self-dimming headlights. It is time for the MGB to have another overhaul/restoration. You have to refresh cars periodically to keep them running well and looking nice. Well I would hang around and say more but it is after 10am and there's a small adventure at a hotel to get to today. Ciao, babies!!!!

04/10/2006

Fair Warning!: MEN I am more than willing to enjoy whatever sexual pleasures you are willing to offer, but it says in our profile to "leave my admittedly delightful rump alone." which is much nicer than "spank me and you die!" but the effect should be much the same. Only it hasn't been. Cat has even said "No, she doesn't like it." to men who ignore him and do it again who then find themself without a partner. To each their own, of course, but unless she specifically asks to be spanked, DON'T. Thank you.

The MGB works well now! Yeeehaw! Zoom, zoom, zoom!

You have to understand - we ask impossible to answer questions because the question we are really asking is not the one we asked. You only have to lie if you answer the question we actually asked. If you answered the question we really wanted answered you wouldn't have to lie. Women are naturally more sibylline than men and we do sooo enjoy playing that delightful game "Confuse-A-Male". But I am merciful. The correct answer to all such questions is (take notes here) : "Darling you are so gorgeous that I am the most fortunate of men and I love you dearly." If you can say that and enfold her into your arms - so much the better! Got that? This has been a test. This has only been a test. If this had been an actual emergency we would have asked a woman. LOL Ciao, babies!!!

04/11/2006

206

Men in chaps YES YES YES!! In fact, and I believe I have posted a similar request before, I think we should have Wet Brief Contests, Men dressing up as firemen, policemen, lifeguards, gladiators, in togas and as cowboys for the women's delight. Hey we do this stuff for you! Fair is fair! So get out there and shake that booty! Full Monties for all the ladies!!! Go men go!!

busy being sibylline and putting something together for opening day of the polo season

TABU may be utterly wonderful but they are up against people whose ideas are set in stone. Those who fear cling ever more tightly to their beliefs seeking some measure of security. I wonder if TABU has sought counsel from The Cottage and/or The Farm? The Cottage is right in town there perhaps they have had their battles as well? Just a thought. Ciao, Babies!!!

04/11/2006
Something different for you all: Arranging her skirts, she straddled my lap facing me on my sofa. She was so beautiful. Her eyes laughed and sparkled. Her lips curved delightfully and when she kissed me so lightly all of the desire I had for her flared up. Delicately kissing my lips over and over making me quiver. When she lifted her face away I became aware of the collar around my neck. I said nothing as she began undoing my shirt buttons and running her hands through my chest hair, caressing me. I stopped her hands at my belt buckle. It was too soon for me. Yes, I wanted her. But between wanting and having there lay issues. A messy past, an uncertain future, and a woman I barely knew

snuggling into my arms as I wore her collar around my neck. There was that ring on her left hand. Where did that put me? Yes I wanted her, who wouldn't?, but I am not a young guy heedless of consequences. No, not tonight. But you know I was kicking myself as I went upstairs to bed after watching her drive off.

What I wanted was not what she could give. What I wanted, she already had. Where did that leave me? Yes, she's a domme' but I haven't seen a whip yet. She seems kind and patient. I like her as a person and I care about her as a friend. But what am I getting myself into? She wants me? A beautiful woman wants me? And here I am somewhat bewildered since I am not a young tall hardbodied hunk who's hung like a horse. I am not bad but she could have any man she really wanted. I am not rich either. She must just like me for some reason. What do I know about women?

I tried to resist but then she was sitting next to me on my sofa. she had my shirt off and she ran her fingertips slowly and lightly up my spine and blew gently on the nape of my neck and lightly licked my ear. Okay, okay, I give in! Take me upstairs to my bed! She did. I did. We did. Still no whips. She doesn't need them. Force of personality, drop dead sexy beauty, razor intelligence, and a skill at seduction that you have to experience to believe makes coercion unnecessary. Yeah, I am her slut. My former reluctance makes me smile.

04/12/2006
All I can say is we let these people in when we don't take the jobs instead. If we had lifestylers on that

committee or board, this protest would never had taken place. You could axe it by simply saying "I have been to such places before. Nothing much happens." then shrug and pass on to more 'worthy' issues. You how committees work, if its boring, or there's no media value in it, they move on.

so okay you don't like prose, hmmm, well let me go and assuage Cat's feelings and I will get back to you on this

Easter is here and so is the big Family Reunion/Work Project! I am going to head north tomorrow evening, after rush hour, and join up with the rest to put a new roof on mom's house. My job, I have be so informed, is to walk around and pick up nails using a magnet on a stick thing. Cat has to stay behind, poor fella, but I know you all will take good care of him while I am gone. Just no more bruises on him okay, dear? Happy, happy, people! Ciao, babies!!

04/13/2006
Hmmm, more TABU comments. Amazing the issues people have when it comes to sex - including us. What one person sees as normal, another sees as licentiousness. To some its a blowjob, to others it is feeding off of the male. Perspectives. If this community leader type person has an issue about swinging then I suggest he not do it.

This from a friend of mine: AND I QUOTE "Personal growth for either wife or husband may well require other intimate friendships with consent and seeking the best for each other. Secondary relationships can serve not only personal growth but also and at the same time serve the marriage itself. Raymond J. Lawrence, an Episcopal chaplain and marriage counselor, observes that transmarital sexual relationships would only be considered "unfaithful" if done for inappropriate motives such as revenge or to hurt the other. But, "the refusal to open oneself to secondary sexual relationships can also be based upon inappropriate reasons. An emotionally immature, religiously self-proving desire for purity and innocence might be one. Another might be the resistance to sufficient autonomy and the persistence in a clinging dependency upon the spouse - which is different from mature interdependency. The high degree of intimacy possible in a good marriage seems to depend in no small measure upon the relative absence of possessiveness and clinging dependency." IBID It all depends upon what you believe. Ciao, babies!!

04/17/2006
Argh! Please do not mention taxes!!! OH MAN THIS IS GONNA HURT!!! Damn, how I hate writing that check! It is such a shame that crucifixes do not ward off the IRS. Have to hang by the phone today so it is just as well that it is raining outside. One of the trees fell last weekend while I was out of town. A big tree. Leaning up against the neighbor's fence but didn't crash through it - the physics must have been just right. Some rope and a chain saw. Rip rip rip! Went out of town to de-roof and then re-roof Mom's house. Feeling like I need a spa day now.

transmarital sexual relationships - I like it!

Look people, we don't bite! You can meet us in perfect safety and we are fun even with our clothes on! So this making a date and then NOT showing up - well it is just sooo not 'happening' ya know? Tsk, tsk, tsk. Such timid people. Not me. Asked my new aunt whom I met for the first time this weekend "Do you swing?" She answered "Yes!" Now is that a kick in the head or what? His 3rd her 4th marriage. Do not ask me what prompted me to ask her because I do not know. Just got this idea. Amazing!! Ciao, babies!!!

04/18/2006
I want you all to welcome my sexcretary T to the office! Very nice man and a hard worker who has already helped me out a lot. When you call, you may speak to him about anything - he sets my schedule after all. WOOT! I am telling you - you have GOT to get you a sexcretary! Next up on the hiring agenda is a assistant! Yes, he knows who he is. As soon as the next contract comes in he's hired, baby! Double WOOT!

Hey! Squirrels!

In any case we are both working very hard so our adventures have been very few. This is unfortunate as we really, really, REALLY enjoy our adventures and would like to encourage you all to mutually participate in as many as possible. The trouble is - whenever I am nice to Cat, he starts looking at me in a highly suspicious manner. Come on now! I do not bite THAT much! Well. Okay. Not much. Lately. Let's move delicately on now. LOL Ciao, babies!!!

04/19/2006

As a woman who simply absolutely likes, enjoys, and adores men - esp teddybears - I sympathize with you. There is plenty of room for all of us in this big wide world. Actively discouraging anyone in particular is not required and certainly not very nice. We are all naked here after all! At least I hope you are *W*. Just lay down right here, baby and leave it all to the not-so-nice lady. LOL

Listening to French jazz music - sounds good - I don't understand a word of it. - but Hey! It swings!

I may have knitted my schedule into a tight knot. Have to skip this year's Upperville Horse and Colt Show but I will be able to make the Potomac Races. Polo opens this year on May 27th. Parties May 18th and June 22nd. Out of Town from June 1st through perhaps the 14th - more or less. Parties and orgies and meets the 20th, 21st, 26th, and 28th of April. May 4th's gone already. Perhaps also the 3rd of May - we will see. HEY! Look, just call us quickly and we will fit you in! *KISS* Ciao, babies!!!

04/20/2006

Sorry to hear about your dad, Smokey but glad he is improving and will soon be home and back on his feet.

I wish they could have 1 designated room where the non-smokers can go when they feel the need to breathe. *WEG*

Not your usual blog today but the ladies and I were very busy having an EXTREMELY DELICIOUS time playing with all of the Cat Toys this afternoon.

212

Wow did certain ladies miss one GREAT time!!
BTW we gave out T-shirts for the guys! Way Kewl!
Blindfolds and scented body oils to the fore and let
no man escape! LOL Ciao babies!!!!

04/21/2006
Turning down unwanted attention is easy. You
simply tap into your 'inner bitch' look the man
straight in the eye and sternly say "We do not suit.
Thank you. Goodbye." Then you leave. Normally -
do NOT run and if you simply must skip for joy at
the happy escape, try to do so out of his line of
sight. Of course it helps if your rep is one that says
you are 'big and bad' but one can borrow the attitude
anytime.

QUOTE: Two drink limit does not mean first and
last. Two drink limit does not mean two kinds of
drinks. Two drink limit does not mean the drinks
can be as large as I like. "No Drinking Of Alcoholic
Beverages" does not imply that a Jack Daniel's ®
IV is acceptable. UNQUOTE

Since my sexcretary is off today, I wonder what
kind of trouble I can get into now that I am without
his supervision? Perhaps I can go and try to recruit
more 'teddybear fancying kittens' to my network?
The party yesterday was MARVELOUSLY
DELICIOUS! The Cat Toys are excellent men! The
ladies are all highly desirable. Everyone was FUN!!
Blindfolds and scented body oils worked very very
well too *W*. The Cat Toys all enjoyed being
'appreciated'. We even gave them t-shirts that said
CAT TOY on them *EG* Ciao, babies!!!!!!!!

04/24/2006

Open Call Group Therapy Session May18th at noon venue tba. Send first name, handle and cell number to YIM kitz238 to get on the list.

Fly down to Mexico? Surely you jest! I barely have enough time to fit everything in as it is let alone taking even a weekend off like that! If even Baltimore is too far, you can imagine that Mexico might as well be out beyond Pluto. Sorry but I have obligations. Like roofing and felling trees around the house. Busy, busy, busy. My shoulder hurts too. OUCH!

I did get into a bit of trouble last Friday as a friend lent me her hubby who gives WONDERFUL massages. Cat wandered in about then too. Then Cat and I went to the Taj and one of my 'prospects' wandered in and met everyone - remember the guy in the suit?- Cat was amused. Lots of fun and games!

Did I mention that those who RSVP yes and yet DON"T show are blacklisted? *EG* The way it has to be, babies! Each 'no-show' means we have eat the hotel room charges for that person. Bad; very, very bad! But we are trying this again. Open Call Group Therapy Session May18th at noon venue tba. Send first name, handle and cell number to YIM kitz238 to get on the list. Women do not go through the Selection Committee but all men do. See the posting under Member Calendar for more information. Ciao, babies!!

04/26/2006

When the califraction of one's livery is imminent, one absquatulates. - absquatulates beats irregardless hands down. Having studied the various 'abusive' terms available - scrophulous, pidiculous, and necrobestial - I can say that if you want to insult someone, use the Latinate form of English. By the time they have looked it up, you will be long gone! Esp if you also do it in the subjunctive! Beware, I have the OED and I know how to use it!

ok G! We'll be good while you are having fun down in Florida. *EG*

Drove my MGB yesterday to a lunch meeting with a lady 'of like mind and personality'. I really really REALLY love that car! Besides I have to begin my tan. L was great! A bright and charming lady who is more merely interested in messing about with men and only men. She even liked my car! Way kewl! Comes from that small town "Flood City" in western PA! Now. If she shares her men and I share my men - what sort of a party will it be? Ciao, babies!!!

04/27/2006

Way too complicated! All I need for my workout is a comely, willing, and naked male...or two. *EG* I am VERY active. As for simple pleasures - sitting next to him on my back deck getting quietly drunk on excellent single malt scotch watching the summer sunset while listening to Janis sing Summertime. Simple but sublime!

Called Frank - left a message

The Commonwealth has been answered! I do so hope that keeps them at bay. Now to tackle the Quickbooks and write my first paycheck! Eeeeek! I am in danger of becoming a 'responsible adult' and an 'employer' !! HELP ME I am losing my youthful waywardness!! Where will it all end? Next thing you know I will be paying a bill as soon as it comes in!! Noooooooooooo!!! Ciao, babies!!

04/28/2006
The time has come the vet has said to bring Ambersandy in, for this and that and to see what kind of shape she's in. Well she's round, and furry, and orange, buff a bit of white - you know, one of the tabbies. BTW she hates going to the vet and always leaves us and the truck smelling bad because cats sweat through their little pink paw pads.
Frank called at 6:11 am. What was he thinking?!?! He will call back circa 12 noon.
Then there's the grocery-getting and housework. Ah, me! Making a list of 'home improvements' that need to be made. And now, a word from our sponsor!
QUOTE: Last night the silken slow sliding down your body finding that which made you quiver and catch your breath in delight slow very slowly twining around your shoulders your waist your loins feeling you against my cheek your skin and fur on my skin until I too quiver and burn with a predatory desire kissing caressing licking hearing your pleasure the black leather cuffs on your wrists the strap around the bedpost restraining your arms kissing up and along nuzzling enjoying you purrrrr bless and be blessed. UNQUOTE.

"Thus ends The First Year!"

Ciao, babies!!